Great things to do Outside

365 AWESOME OUTDOOR ACTIVITIES

Jamie Ambrose

DK

**LONDON, NEW YORK, MELBOURNE,
MUNICH, AND DELHI**

DK LONDON
Project Art Editor Clare Joyce
Project Editors Wendy Horobin,
Ruth O'Rourke Jones, David Summers
Editor Lili Bryant
US Editor Margaret Parrish
Senior Preproduction Producer Ben Marcus
Senior Producer Alice Sykes
Jacket Designer Mark Cavanagh
Jacket Editor Manisha Majithia
Jacket Design Development Manager Sophia MTT
Managing Art Editor Michelle Baxter
Managing Editor Angeles Gavira Guerrero
Publisher Sarah Larter
Associate Publishing Director Liz Wheeler
Art Director Philip Ormerod
Publishing Director Jonathan Metcalf

DK INDIA
Managing Art Editor Sudakshina Basu
Managing Editor Rohan Sinha
Senior Art Editor Mahua Sharma
Art Editors Kanika Mittal,
Shreya Anand Virmani
Editor Suefa Lee
DTP Designers Neeraj Bhatia,
Syed Mohammed Farhan, Bimlesh Tiwari
Preproduction Manager Balwant Singh
Production Manager Pankaj Sharma

First American Edition, 2014
Published in the United States by DK Publishing
4th floor, 345 Hudson Street, New York, New York 10014

14 15 16 17 18 10 9 8 7 6 5 4 3
005-192378-Mar/2014

Published in Great Britain by
Dorling Kindersley Limited.

A catalog record for this book is available
from the Library of Congress.

ISBN 978-1-4654-1685-8

DK books are available at special discounts when purchased in bulk
for sales promotions, premiums, fund-raising, or educational use.
For details, contact: DK Publishing Special Markets, 345 Hudson
Street, New York, New York 10014 or SpecialSales@dk.com.

Printed and bound by Leo Paper Products, China

Discover more at **www.dk.com**

BE SAFE! IMPORTANT NOTE TO PARENTS
Some of the activities in this book require adult supervision. Always
ensure that your child follows instructions carefully and remember to
keep them safe when exploring outside. The Publisher has set out
some basic guidelines on safety see pp.4–5, but it is the responsibility
of every user of this book to assess individual circumstances and
potential dangers of any activity they wish to undertake. The Publisher
cannot accept any liability for injury, loss, or damage to any user or
propery following suggestions in this book.

The Publisher would draw the reader's attention to the
following particular points:

• Plants may be poisonous or protected by law from
picking or uprooting

• Fungi and berries should only be collected for consumption at
reader's own risk since many fungi and some berries are poisonous

• Wild animals may bite or sting – take suitable precautions
and a first aid kit

Contents

How to use this book

This book is full of fun and exciting things to do, from building a den to pressing flowers and trapping bugs. Take it with you wherever you go and you'll find an activity that helps you explore the natural world. It doesn't matter if the book gathers a little dirt along the way—just don't let it gather dust on your shelf.

Photographs and clear step-by-step instructions show you what to do at each stage

Larger pictures show you what your finished projects should look like, so that you can copy them

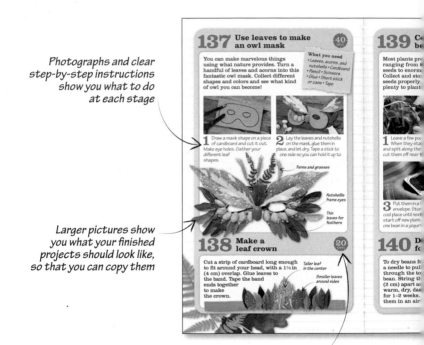

A clock indicates how long you'll spend doing an activity. This does not include any downtime, such as waiting for things to grow or dry.

When exploring, follow all laws and be respectful of nature and of others:
• Plan ahead, be safe, and obey all signs
• Leave property exactly as you found it
• Protect plants and animals and take your litter with you
• Keep dogs on a leash
• Be considerate of wildlife and of other people

And remember—always release the animals you investigate back into the wild (preferably in the place you found them) at the end of an activity.

A "What you need" checklist shows you the equipment you should have ready before you start the activity and the items you will need to collect

Information stamps include top tips to help you complete the projects (green), fun facts (blue), safety tips (pink), and suggestions for alternative things to try (orange)

Activity number—each activity is numbered so you can keep track of what you have done—there's an activity number for every day of the year!

001 Make a seed box

Gather and store seeds and grow your favorite garden plants the following year—for free. Collect seeds when the pods are ripe, dry them, and store them in a special box. Keep the box in a cool, dry place until spring.

Paper seed envelope

Seasonal divider

What you need
- Shoebox, with lid • Wrapping paper
- Tape • Scissors • Cardboard • Paint, markers • Small brown envelopes

1 Wrap the box and lid in wrapping paper. Cut dividers from the cardboard the same width as the box. Paint or mark dividers in seasonal designs.

2 Decorate the envelopes. Draw a picture of the plant on the seed packet. Put your seeds inside.

3 Seal the envelopes. Label each with the seed name and date of collection. Put each in the right section *Sunflower seeds* and close the lid.

002 Fly a seed helicopter

Some trees, such as maple, have winged seeds to travel on the wind. If you find one, hold it by the round part of the wing, throw it straight up in the air, and watch it spin like a helicopter.

Seeds join in middle

Single wing

003 Make a bumblebee nest box

20 MINS

Bumblebees nest in the ground. The queen bumblebee usually tries to find an abandoned mouse or vole hole by tracking the scent of the rodent's nest, but you can help out the bees by building this bumblebee nest box.

What you need
• Trowel • 4 stones
• Flowerpot
• 5 x 5 in (12 x 12 cm) piece of slate • Hay or wood shavings

1 Dig a hole in the ground deep enough to hold the flowerpot. The pot needs to be ceramic, with a central drainage hole.

2 Add hay or wood shavings. This will help the queen to find it because it will smell like a mouse's nest.

Cover keeps out rain

3 Put the upturned flowerpot in the hole, set out the stones in a square shape around it, and place the slate on top to keep out the rain.

004 Plant a bee-friendly garden

15 MINS

Fill your garden with flowering bee-friendly plants such as lavender, buddleias, anemones—anything with nectar-rich flowers. Species that bloom at different times will give bees a constant food source.

Lavender

005 Build a den

Set up a den near a tree in the backyard and you'll have a private hideout—a place to hang out with your friends. Make it waterproof, and you can have sleepovers there when the weather is good.

What you need
- Stakes or poles
- Material: tarpaulins, sacking, and old bedding • Twine or rope • Large tree

1 First, decide where you want your den to be. Building it next to a large tree not only gives you an instant "back wall," but it also provides cover, shade, and stability if the den leans against it or is tied to its trunk or branches.

2 For a simple framework, arrange the stakes in a teepee. Push the bottom ends into the ground, then tie them together at the top with twine.

3 Drape and tie your fabric pieces onto the stakes. You might use all non-waterproof material first, then cover them with a tarpaulin if you want to use the den in wet weather.

Waterproof groundsheet

4 If the ground is damp, lay a waterproof groundsheet or tarp down as a floor. Remember to leave an opening for a doorway!

006 Make a slingshot catapult

Stretch a thick rubber band across a strong, forked stick. Insert a paper ball or dried pea between your thumb and finger and pull back the rubber band. Aim at a can or rock (never at animals or people), and let fly.

007 Thread a flower garland

Fresh flowers are nature's perfect decorating tool. Why not show them off to fantastic effect by making this flower garland? It's ideal for a summer garden party or barbecue. ⚠

What you need
- Fresh flowers: chrysanthemums or marigolds are ideal
- Thin garden wire
- Scissors

1 Snap or cut off the flowers just below the head. Cut a 2½ ft (70 cm) length of wire and twist a loop at one end.

2 Push the unlooped end of wire into the center of the stem and up through a flower. Slide the flower along.

3 Add flowers until the wire is nearly full. Finish with another loop. Make more strands in the same way. Use the loops to hang your garlands.

008 Hang a flower curtain

1 HR

Instead of making curved swags with your garlands, leave them as long strings. Hang the garlands vertically next to each other from a branch to make a magical flowery curtain.

Add ribbons if you like

009 Plant a round pizza garden

45 MINS

You can't grow cheese, pepperoni, or dough, but you can grow many of the plants used as pizza toppings. Plant your favorites in a round container, and add dividers to make a living "pizza."

What you need
- Scissors • 6 foam pizza bases • Waterproof paint
- Trowel • Circular container
- Compost • Pizza plants: basil, tomatoes, oregano, peppers, garlic, onions

1 Paint the pizza bases. You can label them with the names of your pizza plants.

2 Put rocks into the container to provide drainage, then fill the container with compost. Use the dividers to make "slices."

3 Add your plants, filling in any gaps with more compost. Water them well, and water again whenever the soil looks dry.

Onions

010 Grow your own herbs

20 MINS

Choose seeds of your five favorite herbs, such as sage, parsley, dill, basil, and thyme. Sow parsley in an "X" to divide the container into four, then sow the other herbs, one per section. Water well.

Sage

Parsley forms an "X"

011 Build a butterfly bar

45 MINS

Butterflies feed at flowers, sucking up nectar with a long, tubelike structure called a proboscis. Tempt them in with this butterfly bar full of sugary treats.

1 Ask an adult to help you with the first two steps. Peel the banana and slice it into a bowl. Mash it up with the fork.

Banana paste

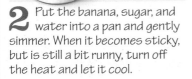

2 Put the banana, sugar, and water into a pan and gently simmer. When it becomes sticky, but is still a bit runny, turn off the heat and let it cool.

3 Punch three holes in the paper plate, thread a piece of string through each one, and tie with a knot. Hang the plate on a branch, spoon on some paste, and wait for butterflies to land.

012 Attract butterflies

30 MINS

Tempt butterflies into your yard by planting their favorite flowers. Buddleia is so popular that it's even called the "butterfly bush." Daisies and lavender are also good choices.

Butterfly feeding at a clover flower

013 Keep a nature-day photo journal

The next time you visit your favorite natural place, make a photo journal of the experience. Whether it's a woodland, a beach, or your local park, taking pictures will help you remember it—and enjoy it later, too.

What you need
- Nature journal or notebook
- Pen or pencil
- Digital camera

My house

1 Start by noting down where you are in your journal, then take a wide shot of the environment, showing landmarks or notable features in the background.

2 Next, focus on the details. If you find a favorite wild flower or insect, take a photo. Look up, look down, and everywhere in between.

3 If you find something you can't identify, note down where it is—in the shade, sun, sandy soil, rich earth—in your journal. Between your notes and the photo record you may be able to identify it when you get home.

Bee on scabious flower

014 Make a nature photo postcard

Take a digital photo of a friend or family member—or get someone to take one of you—enjoying the natural world. Print it, write it, and send it "snail mail" or use it as an e-postcard.

A day among the wild flowers

015 Build a birdbath

20 MINS

You may already be helping birds by putting out food, but birds also need water to survive. Make them a birdbath so they have somewhere to drink and a place to bathe.

What you need
• Shallow bowl • Small stones, pebbles, and shells, rinsed • Clean plastic bottle and cap • Thumbtack • String

1 Put small stones in the bottom of the bowl. Set the bowl on a pedestal near bushes or trees. Add slightly bigger pebbles or shells.

2 Make holes in the bottom of the bottle. Fill the bottle with water, screw on the cap, attach the string, and hang it over the bath.

3 Add water to the bowl. Clean the bowl every few weeks with mild disinfectant to prevent bacterial growth.

Birdbath

Shower

016 Turn a trash can lid into a birdbath

10 MINS

Make sure it doesn't wobble

Set three bricks in a triangle on open, level ground. Put the upturned lid on the bricks. Add a layer of pebbles, especially in the deepest part. Fill with water.

017 Make a potted gift kit

20 MINS

The next time you need a gift for someone special, give this flowerpot kit. Not only will the lucky person be able to enjoy the potted flowers far longer than cut ones, but he or she will have the pleasure of planting them, too!

What you need
- Flowerpot and drip tray • Flower seeds
- Ribbon • A small bag each of gravel and compost

1 Fill two plastic bags—a small one with gravel and a larger one with compost. Tie these with cheerful ribbons.

2 Put the bags and seed packet inside the pot and put the drip tray on top to form a lid.

3 Cut two long lengths of ribbon and lay them out in a cross. Put the pot on top. Tie one ribbon around it first, then tie the other. Bring the ends all together in a bow.

Add seeds or bulbs

Bags of compost and gravel

Add your own design with acrylic paint

018 Give a scented bouquet

10 MINS

Find the most fragrant, sweet-smelling flowers in your garden, such as lavender, roses, and jasmine. Arrange them in a bouquet, tie them with a pretty ribbon, and then give them to someone as a present.

Roses have a sweet scent

019 Make a daisy chain

10 MINS

If you have daisies growing in the yard, then you have everything you need to make a daisy chain. Once you have the hang of it, why not see how many different things you can make from the daisies?

What you need
• Lots of daisies

1 Pick a few daisies with long stems. Use your thumbnail to split the stem of one near the bottom of the stem.

2 Thread another daisy through that hole, then make a split in the second daisy's stem and thread a daisy through that.

3 Keep going until you have a really long chain. Make a garland or crown by carefully threading the first flower head through the last split stem.

020 Blow a dandelion clock

1 MIN

Find a dandelion seed head and try to blow all the seeds away. According to folklore, the number of puffs it takes will tell you the time—so three puffs is 3 o'clock.

Try to blow them all at once

021 Look for space rocks

Every day, about 500 tons of rock from space collides with our planet. Most rocks burn up as shooting stars, but tiny particles often float to Earth. Try this experiment and you may find some micrometeorites.

What you need
- Magnet • Paper cup
- String • Sheet of white paper
- Magnifying glass
- Tweezers

1 Tie a loop of string to the cup, as shown. Put a strong magnet inside. Take this outside and tap it gently on dry ground.

2 When black specks show on the cup base, take it indoors. Put it on the white paper. Remove the magnet. Tap the cup to release the specks.

Tiny particles

3 Use a magnifying glass and tweezers to pick out rounded specks. These could be magnetic iron or nickel micrometeorites.

022 Make a Martian landscape

Put sand in an old baking sheet. Snip steel wool over it. Moisten the sand with salty water and leave for a few days. As the steel wool rusts, the sand turns red, like the soil on Mars.

Martian soil contains a lot of iron

023 Make a fossil mud pie

Professional fossil hunters spend weeks slowly removing layers of soil from fossils so the fossils stay intact. Do you have what it takes to be a fossil hunter? Make a fossil mud pie, swap it with a friend's, and find out!

What you need
- Objects to bury
- Garden soil • Shovel
- Bucket • Mug • Trowel
- Water • Old mixing bowl or large plastic container • Paintbrush
- Tweezers

1 Collect bones, shells, or man-made items like coins to bury. Put three shovelfuls of soil in a bucket. Break the soil up with a shovel, then crumble it with your hands. Remove twigs, stones, or other debris.

2 Add six mugfuls of soil to the bowl. Add half a mugful of water and mix into very thick mud with your hands. Add more water if needed to make a thick, but not runny, mud that will set well.

Brush gently

Slowly reveal your fossil

3 Bury your objects in the mud. Put the bowl in a dry place and let the mud set. Swap your bowl with a friend's and excavate!

4 Carefully remove the soil with the trowel, working from the outside in. Brush away loose soil. Lift fragile objects with tweezers.

024 Hunt for fossils

You can find fossils anywhere—even in the gravel near your home. Look for fossils in stones, on beaches, chalk cliffs, limestone hills, or riverbanks.

Ammonites

025 Press flowers

30 MINS

If you have plenty of flowers in the garden, why not preserve some by pressing them? It's easy to do, and once dried, the flowers can be used to make pretty bookmarks, gift tags, pictures, greeting cards, and more.

What you need
- Flowers and leaves
- Heavy books
- White blotting paper
- Scissors

1 Open a heavy book. Cut a piece of blotting paper about the same size as the open book, fold it in half, then open it again.

2 Lay the paper across the book. Arrange the flowers on the right half, with plenty of space between each.

3 Carefully fold the left side of the paper over the flowers. Close the book over the blotting paper. Put more books on top. Let dry for at least four weeks.

026 Dry and press seaweed

30 MINS

Rinse the seaweed and arrange it on a piece of paper. Set this on newspaper. Put waxed paper on top, wax-side down. Add newspaper, then heavy books. Change the newspaper daily. In 10 days, the seaweed will be dry.

027 Make a butterfly painting

Butterfly wings are usually mirror images of each other. By painting on one side of a piece of construction paper and folding it over, you can mimic this effect to create your own colorful butterfly.

1 Fold the piece of paper in half. Paint a design on one side—you can just blob paint around. Be sure to put some along the fold.

2 Fold the paper in half and press down, rubbing from the center outward. Unfold your painting and let it dry.

3 Your painting should now be almost identical on both sides of the paper. If you like, use pens, pencils, or crayons to add legs, antennae, or even a face to your "butterfly."

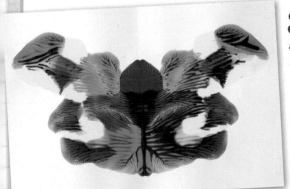

028 Damselfly or dragonfly?

Dragonflies are much larger than their damselfly relatives. Watch the insect land—if its wings are unfolded at rest, it's a dragonfly. At rest, damselflies keep their wings folded up.

Wings out flat
DRAGONFLY

Wings folded

DAMSELFLY

029 Make a bug hotel

Insects need a safe, warm, and dry shelter in the winter. Recycle scrap wood and natural items to make a bug hotel. In the spring, the bugs will repay you by pollinating your plants.

What you need
- Pinecones • Thistles • Drilled wooden blocks • Stakes • Dry branches
- Stems • Wooden frame

1 Ask an adult to help you use scrap wood, such as pallets, to construct a frame for your hotel. Ours is a big rectangle, but yours can be any size or shape.

2 Insert stems, stakes, pinecones, drilled blocks of wood—any items that fit and contain crawl spaces for insects.

3 Pick a site for your hotel. Make sure it's in a sheltered location, facing southeast or southwest, if at all possible.

4 Hang it on a wall, or put it next to one at ground level. Cover all the compartments with wire mesh for more stability if you like.

030 Investigate a tree gall

Galls are growths on leaves, branches, and bark caused by insects, viruses, and fungi. If you see one on a leaf or acorn, carefully cut it open—you could find a developing insect inside.

Oak apple gall was caused by a wasp

031 Carve a Halloween jack-o'-lantern

45 MINS

Jack-o'-lanterns have been made for centuries at Halloween, supposedly to ward off evil spirits. Today, we carve them for fun. See what kind of face you can create on your pumpkin!

What you need
• Ripe, round pumpkin
• Pencil or pen
• Knife • Metal spoon
• Old newspapers
• Bowl • Tealight

1 Spread a layer of newspaper on your work area. Ask an adult to cut around the top of the pumpkin. Remove the lid.

2 Scoop the flesh and seeds into a bowl. You can save the seeds to toast and eat later.

Try different shapes for eyes

3 Draw on a face—triangles are easy to do—then have an adult cut out the pieces. When you're finished, put a tealight inside and let it shine.

032 Hang a pumpkin lantern

10 MINS

Make hanging lanterns from small pumpkins or squashes. Cut designs in the same way as for the jack-o'-lantern, but make a hole in each side so that cord can be tied on for hanging.

FACE LANTERN

DIAMONDS

NIGHT SKY

033 Make a parachute

Make this great parachute with a scrap of cloth, a cup, and thread. Launch it by throwing it straight up in the air. Add a small piece of clay to the cup as a weight and see if it affects how the parachute falls.

What you need
- Round piece of cloth 12 in (30 cm) in diameter
- Darning needle
- Paper cup • Thread

1 Make four holes in the edges of the cloth equal distances apart, like the four points of the compass.

2 Use the needle to push four 12 in (30 cm) threads through four equally spaced holes in the cup's rim, and tie to the cup.

3 Put the cup upside down in the center of the cloth. Use the needle to pull each thread through one of the cloth holes and secure with a knot.

Try it with and without a weight

034 Throw fall leaves in the air

25 MINS → 15 MINS

Throw fall leaves into the air. How many can you catch as they fall? Which shapes fall the slowest? Spray-paint a leaf, put it in the pile, then see who can find it fastest when you throw the leaves.

035 Lay an insect pitfall trap

15 MINS

While humans sleep, many insects are on the move—flying through the night air or crawling over soil. Make a pitfall trap and catch some of these nocturnal creepy-crawlies. Just be sure to let them go again.

What you need
- Trowel • Yogurt cup
- Bait (cheese, fruit, meat) • 4 stones
- Tile or piece of wood 4 in (10 cm) square

1 Dig a hole in soft ground and bury the cup so that its rim is level with the soil. Pack soil around the cup's edges. Add some bait.

2 Put the stones on the ground around the trap and place the tile on top to make a rainproof roof.

Soil packed around edges

Trap in place

3 Leave the trap overnight. Dig up the trap to view your catch. Note down what you've caught, and try again.

036 Lift logs to find insects

5 MINS

Lift a log to see underneath. Ants, beetles, woodlice, and centipedes may be living there. Put the log back safely.

Fern

Moss

037 Make a kite

Flying a kite is a great way to have fun in the summer. You just need an open space that's free of trees and overhanging wires. Add a breeze and your kite, and you're ready for takeoff.

What you need
- Split stakes or basket-weaving reeds
- Glue • Tissue paper
- Cotton thread
- Stapler • Kite string

Don't make it too narrow

Decorate your kite

1 Soak the stakes overnight. Tie them to form a frame. Put glue on the bottom half. Lay the frame glue-side down on tissue paper.

2 Cut around the frame, leaving a 2 in (5 cm) border. Snip the border, fold it over, and glue down. Repeat with the other half.

Attach a long line to the knot

3 Cut two pieces of string, one slightly longer and the other wider than the kite. Knot them together in the middle then tie the ends to the frame.

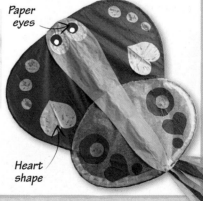

Paper eyes

Heart shape

038 Test your kite-flying skills

30 MINS

Bridle line

Kite string

Put your back to the wind, hold up the kite by the bridle line with one hand, let it catch the breeze, then let out the line. As the kite moves away, pull on the line to make it climb.

039 Reveal leaf skeletons

1 DAY

Deciduous leaves have veins that fan out from a large midrib attached to the stalk. The veins carry food to and from leaf cells. Remove the soft parts of the leaf to reveal its "skeleton" framework.

What you need
• Fallen leaves • Rubber gloves • Saucepan
• 1 quart water
• 3 tbsp washing soda
• Paper towels

1 Ask an adult to help. Add the water and washing soda to the saucepan. Heat until the mixture starts to boil.

2 Remove the pan from the heat. Carefully drop the leaves into the solution. Let them soak for several hours.

Central midrib

3 Wearing the gloves, put the pan under cold running water and rinse the leaves thoroughly. Washing reveals the veiny skeleton. Dry off with paper towels.

Network of veins

> Be careful not to splash hot washing soda on your skin.

040 Take leaf rubbings

10 MINS

Put a leaf onto a smooth surface and cover it with white paper. Hold the paper down, rub over the leaf with a crayon or soft colored pencil. Label each rubbing.

Central midrib

Vein network

041 Make new lavender plants

20 MINS

Don't buy new plants every year! Instead, take cuttings from an old plant and use the cuttings to make new plants. Snip off lavender shoots in late summer, and you'll have several new plants by the spring.

What you need
- Lavender plant
- Small pots • Cutting compost • Scissors
- Plastic bag • Water
- Watering can

1 Find some new growth and cut the stem at an angle just below a leaf. Trim it to 4 in (10 cm). Fill a pot with compost.

2 Remove the lowest leaves until about four remain. Push the cutting into the pot, water it, and let it drain.

New plant

Plastic bag

3 Cover the pot with a bag. Put it in a light place, out of direct sunlight. When new leaves form, move the plant into a new pot.

042 Make herb oil

30 MINS

Cut rosemary sprigs, wash them, and pat them dry with paper towels. Lightly crush the sprigs. Put them in a dry, sterilized bottle (ask an adult to help). Fill the bottle with olive oil, and use it after a week.

Fresh rosemary

Rosemary in oil

043 Plant a hanging basket

1 HR

A hanging basket is really a garden in miniature. Make your own and you can choose the colors and types of plant you want to put in it. Keep it well watered and it should give you weeks of colorful blooms.

Hang it from a strong chain

Primulas and pansies are colorful

What you need
- Wire hanging basket • Sphagnum moss • Plastic trash bag
- Plants • Compost

1 Line the basket with a thick layer of moss, then cut a piece of a trash bag to fit the basket and line it with this. Trim the edges of the liner level with the moss.

2 Make holes around the bottom and, working from the outside, insert some plants roots-first. Fill the bottom with potting compost.

3 Put more plants around the sides and on top, filling gaps with compost. Water the basket and hang it where it is on display and you can water it easily.

044 Make a hanging flower ball

45 MINS

Push a wire through a ball of floral foam. Twist a loop at the top and tie a ribbon to it. Wrap the other end around a small twig for support. Hang, and push the flowers into the foam.

Pack flowers together

Cut stems to 1 in (2.5 cm)

045 Make a shell showcase

The next time you visit a beach and collect shells, why not show them off in this easy-to-make showcase? Be sure to rinse and dry your shells first, then identify them and make labels to go in your showcase.

What you need
- Construction paper
- Pen or pencil
- Ruler
- Scissors
- Tape • Labels

1 Draw and cut a 16 x 12 in (40 x 30 cm) rectangle from construction paper. Mark a 1 in (2.5 cm) margin along all sides.

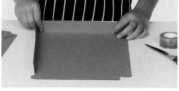

2 Cut into the corners. Fold along the margin to make four sides. Tape the corners. Cut eight strips of paper 1 in (2.5 cm) wide.

3 Fix four strips in the box with tape. Snip almost through the other strips to make compartments. Tape in place.

Identify and label your shells

046 Try beach long jump

Take advantage of a sandy beach to try your skills in the long jump. Draw a line—this is your jump line and you're not allowed to go over it. Take a good run up to it and jump! Try again and see if you can go even farther.

047 Keep a nature journal

Good naturalists keep a journal. Making notes on what you see, hear, and smell when nature-watching helps you remember observations. Include sketches, photos—even leaves, feathers, and flowers.

What you need
• Blank notebook or notepad • Pencil, pen, watercolors, or paints of your choice • Tape • Binoculars

1 Go out and watch a plant, bird, or animal. Note down its appearance, behavior, and surroundings. Use all your senses. What can you hear? See? Smell?

2 Sketch your subject—note colors and distinctive marks. Tape any finds, such as leaves, to your journal pages.

Don't forget your hat!

3 Come back at other times of the year and record any changes.

Leaf specimen

048 Start a leaf collection

Keep a record of trees and bushes by collecting their leaves. Find as many types as you can, tape or glue them onto paper, then identify them.

Fall leaves add color

049 Make a water-balloon piñata

20 MINS

A piñata is usually a container filled with treats that fall out when it is hit by a blindfolded player and breaks open. Try this hot-weather version—the surprise "treat" is a soaking!

What you need
- Water balloons • Funnel • Water
- Foam bat or cardboard tube
- Strong twine or rope • Blindfold

1 Ask an adult to help you tie the twine or rope between two points so that it is about 2–3 ft (0.6–1 m) above the players.

2 Hold the neck of a balloon over the funnel and fill it slowly with water. Tie it off in a knot. The fuller the balloon, the easier it is to burst.

3 Tie each balloon to another length of twine. Add as many balloons as the twine can hold. Tie the balloons to the middle of the rope from step 1.

4 Blindfold the first player, who takes one swing. Blindfold the next player, and continue until all the balloons have burst.

050 Hit targets with water balloons

20 MINS

Set up some targets—these can be plastic bowls, buckets, hoops, or soda bottles. Fill some water balloons, tie them off, and see who can hit the most targets.

Try not to get splashed!

051 Create a flower flick book

30 MINS

Make a flick book of a seed sprouting and you can watch it "growing" whenever you like! Draw a different growth stage in the same place on each page—these act like movie frames when you flick the pages.

1 Fold each piece of paper in half, then in half again, to make four equal squares. Cut them out and staple together.

2 Make your first drawing. A flowerpot is easy to trace onto the other sheets.

Flick the pages to see your "movie"

3 Draw a different growth stage on each page. Show the seedling break the ground, sprout leaves, then flower. Flick to watch your plant "grow."

052 Trim a grass hairstyle

10 MINS

Plant some decorative grass in a flowerpot. Glue on a face, then try out different "hairstyles" on your plant person as the grassy hair grows.

Leave it long or cut it short

053 Take a footprint plaster cast

1 HR

Many wild animals only come out at night, to avoid predators. Often they leave signs of their presence in the form of tracks—and you can preserve these to keep a record of their visits.

What you need
- Posterboard strip 10 x 1½ in (25 x 4 cm) • Water
- Paper clips • Mixing bowl
- Plaster of Paris
- Spoon • Toothbrush

Match up the print

1 Find tracks in soft mud or wet woodland soil. Choose clear ones with the best outlines.

2 Make a ring with posterboard. Secure it with a paper clip. Push the ring into the soil around the track. Mix the plaster until smooth and pour it in the ring.

3 Let set for 30 minutes until it's hard enough to lift. Take it home and let it dry for 24 hours. Brush off any dirt, then use a guide to identify the animal.

054 Identify animal droppings

5 MINS

Black, tube-shaped droppings, or "scat," might belong to a fox. Thin, black tubes could be from a cat. Pellet types are probably from deer or rabbits.

FOX

DEER

RABBIT

WILDCAT

055 Build a birdwatching blind

40 MINS

Wild creatures, including birds, are naturally shy of humans. Making a blind will allow you to watch the animals in your yard without letting them know you're there.

What you need
• 8 stakes • String
• Scissors • Dark-green mesh or netting • Leafy branches • Binoculars
• Clothespins

1 Make the blind frame: Tie the stakes together with string to form a tentlike structure. Tie them tightly to prevent wobbling.

2 Drape the mesh over the frame. Attach it to the frame with clothespins so it doesn't flap in the wind.

3 Poke branches through the mesh to camouflage the blind. Cut peepholes at eye level. Take your binoculars inside and see who shows up!

Birds only see binoculars

Make notes and sketches—they'll help you learn more about animals.

056 Camouflage yourself

5 MINS

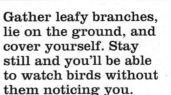

Gather leafy branches, lie on the ground, and cover yourself. Stay still and you'll be able to watch birds without them noticing you.

Brace yourself on your elbows

057 Make a grapefruit geode

2 HRS

Geodes are dull-looking rocks, but crack one open and you'll find sparkling crystals inside. Make a geode by using a grapefruit as the "rock" and a chemical called alum for the crystals.

What you need
- Grapefruit • Spatula
- Foil • Plaster of Paris
- Goggles • Gloves • Alum
- Hot water • Food coloring
- Measuring cup and scales

1 Remove the flesh from half a grapefruit; line the peel with foil. Mix a cupful of plaster in a bowl; follow package instructions.

2 Let the plaster stand until thick, then use the spatula to spread a thick layer over the foil. Put on goggles and gloves.

3 Sprinkle in some alum and let it harden. In a measuring cup, add ½ cup alum and some food coloring to 1¼ cups hot water. Stir well and let cool.

4 Fill the grapefruit with the solution. Over the next week, add any leftover solution. Leave your geode to dry into crystals, then remove the grapefruit peel.

058 Make slime

15 MINS

Pour 1 cup cornstarch into a bowl. Add a few drops of green food coloring to ½ cup of water. Slowly stir into the cornstarch. Add more cornstarch and roll the mixture into a ball. When you stop, it "melts" between your fingers.

Slime becomes sticky and stretchy

059 Make a pinecone wreath

The next time you're outdoors, pick up some pinecones. They're great for making decorations, such as this wreath. Add flowers, nuts, ornaments, and glitter to give it a festive look.

What you need
- Grapevine, raffia, or willow wreath
- Floral wire • Wire cutters • Selection of pinecones

1 Gather enough cones that are roughly the same size. Get an adult to cut the wire for you. Wrap a piece of wire around the base of each cone and twist the wire. Leave two tails so you can attach cones to the wreath.

Small cones are best

Fix wires to the wreath

2 Start by putting cones all around the edge of your wreath. Tie them in with the wire. Once the circle is complete, fill in with more cones.

Add glitter

3 Add dried flowers, nuts, or ribbon if you like. Attach a loop of wire to the back so you can hang the wreath.

060 Create a pinecone animal

Make a pinecone mouse. Cut ears out of felt and glue them to a long acorn. Draw or paint on eyes, a nose, and a mouth. Glue the acorn head to the top of a pinecone. Add a piece of string to make a tail.

Cone body

Maple seed feet

061 Make some bird food

Putting food out for birds is a great way to tempt them into your yard. Good-quality food also keeps them healthy during the winter when wild food is scarce.

What you need
• 2 oz (60 g) lard • 4 oz (125 g) mix of unsalted nuts, oats, birdseed, grated cheese, brown bread crumbs • Small stick
• Yogurt cup • Scissors • Mixing bowl • Wooden spoon • Saucepan

1 Mix the scraps and seeds in a bowl. Ask an adult to melt the lard in a saucepan over low heat. Pour it over the scraps. Stir well.

2 Spoon the mixture into the cup. Push in the stick, and let set.

Stick handle

Birdseed

3 Once the mixture sets hard, pull it out of the cup by the stick. Roll it in more birdseed. Tie a piece of string to the stick, then hang it up outside.

062 Make different types of bird food

Push the lard mix into a fir cone and hang it once set. String nuts and nut shells with a needle. Hang a coconut half from string. When the coconut is eaten, fill it with lard mix.

063 Bobbing for apples

20 MINS

Apple bobbing is a game traditionally played at Halloween or at harvest-time, but you can play it any time you have enough apples—and some friends who don't mind getting wet!

What you need
• Apples • A big bowl or tub—anything deep enough to bob your head into
• Sturdy table • Water • Towels

1 Put the bowl or tub on a sturdy table that's about waist-high. Fill it with cool (not cold) water three-quarters full.

2 Float several apples in the water. You want them to move around—this makes the game more challenging.

3 Put your hands behind your back. Have someone say "Go!" Try to grab an apple with your mouth within 30 seconds. Then it's the next player's turn.

064 Juggle apples

1 HR

Hold an apple in each hand. Throw apple one up and across to hand two. Before you catch it, throw apple two under and across to hand one. Catch apple two, and repeat until perfect.

Once you master juggling two apples, try three!

065 Bury a beetle bucket

Many beetles make their homes on the moist forest floor amid decaying wood and leaves. Sadly, some are vanishing due to habitat loss. This beetle bucket could help your local beetles survive.

What you need
- Plastic bucket
- Craft knife • Stones
- Bark chippings
- Shovel • Logs
- Garden soil

1 Cut 1 in (3 cm) holes in the sides and bottom of the bucket for entryways. Choose a location that won't be disturbed.

2 Bury the bucket in a deep hole. Put large stones in the bottom, then add one or two logs (oak is best); stand them on end.

3 Fill the bucket with bark chippings, then a little soil. Female beetles will lay their eggs on the logs, and the larvae will eat the wood as it decays.

4 Put some logs on top of the bucket to mark the site and leave the area undisturbed. Other beetles will use the logs on top, as well as those in the bucket.

066 Tell a bug from a beetle

There are over 350,000 different types of beetle. Most have hard wing cases that hide their hind wings. Their mandibles are used for chewing food instead of sucking up liquid like a bug does.

Antennae
Mandible
Thorax
Foreleg
Hard wing case
Leg joint
Head
BEETLE

067 Start a rock collection

1 HR

A rock collection is easy to start—rocks are all around you. First check out the rocks in your driveway, garden, or on beaches or riverbanks. Try to identify your favorites, then compare them with ones you find farther away.

What you need
- A keen eye
- Field guide to rocks and minerals
- Magnifying glass

1 Divide your collected rocks into groups. Think about color, size, or where you collected them.

2 Use a magnifying glass to inspect your rock. Is it smooth or grainy? Does it contain crystals? Also look for layers, veins, bubbles, or cracks.

3 Make a display case or specimen tray for your best finds. As you identify them, add a label in each compartment so that you know what rock it is. You might choose to have a tray for crystals and another for green minerals, for instance.

Add labels to each of your specimens

068 Make a specimen tray

15 MINS

Cut posterboard into a square. Cut small squares out of each corner to make side flaps. Fold up each flap and tape together. Cut out small boxes to tape inside as compartments.

Fold up and tape sides

069 Make herb and flower ice cubes

Freezing plants is one of the easiest ways to preserve them for future use. You can give lemonade an extra-special touch with flower-filled ice cubes, or chop up summer herbs for use in the winter.

What you need
- Edible flowers (violas or borage) or herbs (mint, parsley, lemon verbena) • Water
- Ice-cube tray

1 Choose the flowers and herbs you want to freeze. Chop green herbs, or use just one leaf per cube. Use one small whole flower in each ice cube.

2 Put your herbs or flowers into each cube and fill with water. Try star-shaped or other ice-cube shapes to make even more of an impact.

3 Put the tray into the freezer. When frozen, use the flower and leaf cubes in summer drinks. Keep the chopped herbs for soups and stews.

Whole flower head

Chopped herbs

Frozen flower

070 Make it frosty

Put crushed ice into a glass. Add salt to melt it. As the ice melts, it cools the glass, and water in the air forms frost crystals that cling to the outside.

Ice and salt inside

Frost crystals

071 Take mushroom spore prints

Fungi produce white, yellow, or black spores. Single spores are hard to see, but you can take a print of a whole mushroom. Use lighter or darker posterboard if the print is hard to see.

What you need
- Mature mushroom (from supermarket)
- Colored posterboard
- Glass bowl • Artists' fixative spray

1 Place a mushroom cap, gill- or pore-side down, on a piece of posterboard. Put the bowl over the cap to protect it from drafts.

2 Leave overnight, then carefully lift the cap from the posterboard. You should now have a spore print.

White spore print

3 Be careful not to touch your print or it will smudge. Spray the print with fixative in a ventilated room or outdoors, to stop the spores from rubbing off.

072 Make stamps with mushrooms

Cut a mushroom cap in half. Dip it into paint or ink and press it gently onto a sheet of paper. By linking the stamps, you can create patterns and different designs.

Use two colors

073 Decorate your garden with butterflies

Gardening isn't all about plants. It's a chance to have fun and be creative, too. Make these colorful foil butterflies and add some sparkle to garden borders.

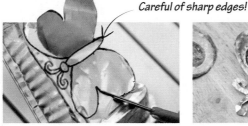

Careful of sharp edges!

1 Use a black marker to draw your butterfly design on the bottom of a container. Cut out the design with a pair of scissors.

2 Press a ballpoint pen head into the design to make a raised pattern. Add color using the colored markers. Let dry.

Plant marker

Bird design

3 Put glue on a stick and press down until it's secure. Let it dry. Find the best place in your garden to show off your artwork!

074 Make pebble pets

25 MINS

Gather some pebbles and wash them. Glue small pebbles to larger ones to make frogs and pigs. Use felt ears and a string tail to make a mouse. Paint them and add googly eyes.

STONE FROG

PEBBLE PIG

MOUSE

075 Go on a nature hunt

40 MINS

You don't need to live in a forest to have a nature hunt. With a little observation, you can find lots of animals and plants in your own backyard. Get your friends together and see who finds what.

What you need
• Hunt checklists—as many as there are hunters
• Pencils or pens

1 Make a list of what you think you might find. Put a box next to each potential find so you can check it off. Start with small creatures—ants and woodlice—or common plants, like clover.

2 Don't forget that nature is all around you, all the time. You might hunt for specific birds, animals, or insects, or you may want to focus on different types of tree, or even clouds.

3 Hunt bugs under rocks or logs. Look for birds on the ground or in trees. Use all your senses—is there a flower scent on your list? Set a time limit. See who can check the most boxes.

Fill in your checklist as you go

076 Lie down and listen

15 MINS

Lie down outdoors on a grassy hill or under a tree. Close your eyes and keep as still as you can. What do you hear? Trees creaking in the wind? Squirrels chattering? Birdsong? Just listen...

What sounds can you hear?

077 Make leaf flowers

15 MINS

When can one plant turn into another? When you transform garden leaves into these beautiful long-stemmed "roses." It's a pretty way to recycle fallen leaves if they're not too dry.

What you need
- Maple leaves
- A stick
- Thin garden wire
- Wire cutters or scissors

1 Hold a smaller leaf by the stem, vein-side up. Fold the top down to meet the stem, then fold in the sides to make a "bud."

2 Take another leaf, fold it over, then wrap it around the bud. Hold the leaf stems against the stick as you repeat this. **Leaf "petal"**

3 Keep adding leaves until your flower is the size you want, then wrap wire around the leaf stems to attach them to the stick. Make several for a "bouquet."

078 Stencil a ripening fruit

1 MIN

If you have fruit trees in your yard, find a fruit, such as an apple, that is full-sized but not yet ripe. Put a sticker shape on it. As the fruit ripens, the area under the sticker will stay pale.

Smiley face

079 Make a weather front

When a warm and a cool mass of air meet, they create a boundary, or "front" between them. You can't see this happening in air, but you can make a front in a jar to see how it works.

What you need
- Glass jar • Pitcher
- Very hot (not boiling) water • Cold water
- Green food coloring
- Thermometer

1 Fill the jar just over half-full with very cold water. Fill the pitcher with hot water. Add a few drops of food coloring. Stir.

Hold the thermometer carefully

Test the temperatures of the layers

"Weather front"

2 Tip the jar of cold water so that the water is close to the rim. Now slowly pour the green hot water down the jar's neck.

3 The warm green water forms a layer above the cold, heavier water. The area where they meet acts like a weather front.

080 Make a rainbow

Make a rainbow in your backyard. Stand with the Sun behind you. Set the hose on fine spray and slowly move it around until you see a rainbow appear.

Water droplets reflect and split sunlight into colors

081 Build your own barometer

As air gets hotter or colder, it causes shifts in the air pressure, which impacts weather patterns. Build a barometer to measure how the pressure changes in the air—and you can also predict the weather.

1 Cut off most of the round part of the balloon and stretch it tightly over the bowl. Attach it securely with tape.

2 Slit the end of one straw, push it inside the other straw, and tape together. Tape one end to the middle of the balloon.

3 Using your marker and ruler, draw a series of lines ¼ in (6 mm) apart on a folded piece of posterboard. Stand the scale by the end of the pointer.

4 Check the scale every few hours to see if the pointer has moved with changes in the air pressure. Up indicates clear weather; down shows wet weather.

082 Measure hailstones

Center a square block of 1-in (2.5-cm) thick foam on a large sheet of heavy foil, dull side up. Fold the foil over the edges and tape in place. Put the pad out when it hails and measure the dents.

Dull side up

Large hailstone dent

083 Make your own fertilizer

Weeds can help your garden grow if you turn them into fertilizer to feed the plants you really want. Even pesky weeds contain nutrients that are good for another plant's health. Don't throw them away!

What you need
- Bucket • Rubber gloves • 2 bricks
- Compost weeds
- Water • Stick or stake as a stirrer

Large bucket

1 Put on your rubber gloves and gather a bunch of compost weeds, such as nettles, comfrey, docks, and horsetails. Shake off any soil and put them, roots and all, into a large bucket.

2 Weigh down the plants with bricks. Fill the bucket with water and stir it weekly. This part can get smelly!

3 After 3–5 weeks you'll have a gooey mass. Dilute it with water (1 part goo to 10 parts water) and use it weekly to water your plants. See how they grow!

084 Make leaf mold

20 MINS

Put fallen leaves in a plastic garbage bag. When the bag is nearly full, spray the leaves with water. Tie the bag, make some air holes, and put it in a shady spot. After a year, spread the leaf mold on your garden.

085 Make a grapefruit bug catcher

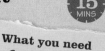
15 MINS

Leaf litter and soil are home to slugs, insects, spiders, worms, and other different types of invertebrate. Use this grapefruit trap to see how many you can find.

⚠️

What you need
- Grapefruit • Spoon
- Notebook or digital camera • Pencil
- Paintbrush • Small plastic container

1 Ask an adult to cut the grapefruit in half. Use the spoon to scoop out the flesh (you can eat this later).

2 Put the grapefruit halves, upside down, on the ground in different sheltered places and leave them out overnight.

3 Turn over the skins. Use the paintbrush to push the animals gently into the container so you can identify them. Then let them go.

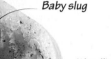

Baby slug

Woodlouse

Leaf litter

086 Be a bug detective

5 MINS

Use a magnifying glass to study insects up close. How many body parts do they have? How many legs? Can you see any pincers or spines?

Leaves let bugs feel safe

Jar lets you get close

087 Make a bubble wand

20 MINS

You may have seen bubble-wand performers in a park or at a street fair creating huge bubbles. Now you can do the same by making this giant bubble wand and bubble mixture.

What you need
• Wire hanger
• Dishwashing liquid
• Glycerine
• Large bowl
• Plastic wrap • Tray

1 Pull the hanger into a circle. In a bowl, mix two parts glycerine to 15 parts dishwashing liquid. Add 15 parts of water slowly. Stir gently.

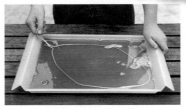

2 Cover the bowl and let the mixture rest for 2–3 days—the longer, the better. Pour it into a waterproof tray.

3 Dip your wand into the mixture, then swish it slowly and smoothly through the air. Make a number of wands to create different-sized bubbles.

088 Blow bubbles with your fingers

1 MIN

If the bubble mixture is thick enough, you can use your own fingers as a wand. Just put your thumb and index finger together in a circle shape, dip in bubble mixture, and blow.

See how large you can make your bubbles!

089 Plant a Wild West garden

Saddle up and give a low container a touch of the Wild West, with prickly cacti and other desert plants. Because their stems store water, cacti can survive if you forget to water them.

What you need
- Container • Gravel
- Cactus compost
- Spoon • Trowel
- Tongs • Gloves
- Cacti • Sand • Water

1 Fill the bottom of the container with a thin layer of gravel. Add 1–2 in (2–5 cm) of compost. Dig holes for your cacti.

2 Wearing gloves, take a cactus from its pot. Use tongs to plant it. Push the soil down around it with a spoon.

3 Plant the other cacti the same way. Lightly water the soil with lukewarm water. Add model figures to create a scene.

090 Make a miniature garden

Fill a jar lid with paper towels or cotton. Dampen it with water. Drop on cress seeds and tiny pieces of gravel. Put in a model animal figurine. Your "cress forest" will grow around it.

Cress plants

Model animal

091 Help a bird build a nest

15 MINS

All birds need a place to raise their young. Building a nest takes a lot of time and energy, but you can help the birds by putting out some of the things they need to make a home.

A nest takes shape

What you need
- 6 shallow dishes • Mud • Moss
- Twigs or pine needles • Straw, grass, dead leaves • Fur, hair, cotton
- Short pieces of string or yarn

1 Fill each bowl with one type of material. Put them in a visible but sheltered place where birds can see them.

2 Keep watch on the bowls from a distance. Do some birds prefer one material more than another?

Mud

Pieces of yarn

Cotton

092 Listen to the dawn chorus

15 MINS

Birds sing all year long, but dawn in spring is when they make the most noise, as males try to find mates and warn off rivals. Get up early to hear them, though—they can start singing at 4 a.m.!

093 Make an anemometer

Wind speed is measured with an anemometer, which rotates as the wind blows. Make this simple anemometer, count the number of turns, and you can figure out wind speed for yourself.

What you need
- 4 small paper cups
- Small paper plate • Pen
- Ruler • Pencil with eraser
- Thumbtack • Double-sided tape • Colored tape

1 Use the ruler and pen to mark an X on the paper plate. Put a band of colored tape around one of the cups.

2 Tape each cup to the plate, facing the same way, so that the center sits at the end of a line.

3 Pin the center of the plate to the eraser so the plate turns easily. Hold the anemometer in the wind. Count the turns the banded cup makes in a minute.

10 turns a minute = roughly 1 mph (1.6 kph)

094 Have a raindrop race

The next time it rains, have a raindrop race with a friend. Each of you chooses a large raindrop at the top of a window. The raindrop that reaches the bottom first wins!

See which raindrop wins

095 Make a feather crown

From Native Americans to Polynesian islanders, people all over the world use feathers to make headdresses. You can, too, with a bit of willow and feathers you've found in the countryside.

What you need
- Feathers
- Long pieces of flexible willow or wisteria vine

1 Make a circle of willow that fits your head. Weave the ends underneath each other to hold the circle together.

2 Wrap more stems or vines in and around the circle. Push the ends beneath the stems to secure in place.

3 Gently push the feather quills in between the stems. Put the largest one at the front and the smaller ones around the sides.

Large feather in front

096 Write with a quill pen

Ask an adult to cut a feather into a flat point with a small slit up the middle. Hold the quill at 45°, dip it into ink or food coloring, and tap off any excess. Write as lightly as you can. Dip and repeat.

097 Build a log-pile home

Rotting wood is important for wildlife, and there is a lot going on in a log pile. It provides food for many animals and insects, and some animals hibernate there in winter. Once built, don't disturb a log pile.

What you need
- Shovel
- Logs and sticks
- Bark, leaves, and ivy plants

1 Pick a shady corner that's out of the way—dappled shade is best. Dig a shallow pit. Pile up the logs, the biggest at the bottom.

2 Put the smaller sticks on top, crisscrossing them as you go. Fill any spaces with leaves, bark, pinecones, or stones.

3 Plant an ivy vine and trail it across the top of the pile to help keep in moisture. Your log pile will now make a warm, safe home for small creatures.

Lichens, mosses, and fungi also grow on log piles and provide food for bugs.

098 Make a maze for woodlice

Use building bricks to make a maze that has a T-junction. Put in some woodlice and let them wander around. Add a brick to make them turn right, then let them choose. Most will turn to the left!

Building bricks

Woodlouse

099 Make a mistletoe ball

Ivy and mistletoe are traditional Christmas decorations that will look fantastic in this "kissing ball." You can probably find ivy in the yard and buy mistletoe at a garden center.

Apple strung on wire

Wire frame

1 Ask an adult to help you make a sphere out of the floral wire. Either twist or tape the wires together.

2 Suspend the apple in the center of the sphere on a separate wire. Push it through the apple and twist to hold. Weave ivy all through the sphere. Add mini ornaments if you like. Attach a bunch of mistletoe to the bottom, add ribbons, and hang.

Ivy hides the wire frame

100 Make a festive bough

Find a bare branch from the yard and ask an adult to help you spray-paint it silver. Suspend it from wire over a doorway. Hang lightweight decorations on it for some added Christmas cheer.

Make it look festive

101 Spread seed hitchhikers

Plants spread seeds in many ways. Many "hitchhike" on passing birds, insects, and animals—including humans. After your next nature walk, see what seeds may have come home with you.

What you need
- Metal baking sheet
- Oven mitts • Seed compost • Knife or screwdriver • Plastic wrap • Watering can

1 Preheat the oven to 200°F (100°C). Fill the baking sheet with compost and bake it for 30 minutes to kill any hidden seeds.

2 Remove the sheet from the oven with oven mitts. Let it cool. Use a screwdriver to scrape your shoe soles over the compost.

3 Water the compost with a fine spray. Cover with plastic wrap. Set the tray on a sunny windowsill. Any hitchhiking seeds should sprout in 10 days.

Shoots grow toward the light

Grass seedling

Compost

102 Plant a sock

10 MINS

Put some old socks over your shoes and take a walk around the yard. Remove the socks, put them in a foil sheet, add compost, and water lightly. See what plants spring up!

Cotton or wool socks are best

103 Play a flying disk game

Try throwing and catching a flying disk, then play a game of "Ultimate." Pass the disk to your teammates to catch it inside the other team's end zone—but no running when you have the disk!

1 To master the backhand throw, grip the disk so that your index finger is on the rim, your thumb is on top, and the rest of your fingertips are just touching the underside.

2 Standing sideways, face your friend. Curl your wrist toward your body, with your elbow pointing up and out. Keep the disk level with your waist to make it fly straight.

3 Quickly fling your arm out, flicking or "snapping" your wrist and releasing the disk when your arm is almost fully extended.

4 To play Ultimate, divide into two teams. Mark two end zones. You score when you catch the disk in the other team's zone.

104 Paper kick-ups

Scrunch scrap paper into a ball. See how long you can keep it in the air without using your hands. Bounce it with your knees, ankles, or head like a soccer player would do—anything goes, except hands!

105 Create a pressed flower picture

30 MINS

Pressed flowers are pretty to look at by themselves, but put several together and you can turn them into a picture. Make this bouquet and hang it on your wall so you can enjoy it all year round.

What you need
- Pressed flowers
- Tweezers • Paper
- Scissors • Clear self-adhesive film
- Toothpick
- Glue • Bottle tops

1 Cut a piece of white paper the size you want your picture to be. Arrange the flowers using tweezers.

2 Pour glue in a bottle top. Use a toothpick to put a tiny drop where you want to glue a flower. When ready, cut the film the same size as the paper.

3 Peel off the backing and carefully place the film over the picture. Press down gently. Your picture is ready to frame.

106 Hang flowers to dry

15 MINS

Remove any damaged leaves from the flowers. Tie the flowers into small bunches with string and hang them upside down in a warm, dry place for 1–2 weeks. They're ready when dry to the touch.

Dry seed heads, too

107 Make a leaf wreath

20 MINS

You can make a wreath at any time of year by using leaves. Choose green ones in spring, or gather fallen ones later in the year—they'll be more brittle, so be gentle!

What you need
- Garden wire cut to the size you want your wreath to be (ask an adult to help)
- Leaves

1 Twist a loop at one end of the wire to hold the leaves. Carefully push the other end through the center of a leaf.

2 String other leaves in the same way, pushing them down to meet the first one. Keep them facing the same way.

3 When you've used all the leaves, put the other end of the wire through the loop. Pull it gently into a circle and use the excess wire to hang it.

108 Hang leaf bunting

10 MINS

Choose prettily shaped or colored leaves from your yard. Tie a piece of twine between two branches, or use thumbtacks to tack a line to a shed door. Hang the leaves with clothespins.

Festive leaves on a line

109 Compare leaf structure

20 MINS

All plants have leaves, but have you ever noticed how different leaves are? A willow tree's are long and slender. An oak's are lobed. A pine tree's are needle-shaped, while a holly's have spiny edges. Learn about trees in your yard.

What you need
• The leaves in your yard or nearby park

1 First, see if the leaf shape is simple or compound. A simple leaf has just one leaf to a stem, like an oak's. A compound leaf has several leaflets coming off a central stem, like the vine called Virginia creeper.

2 How are the leaves arranged? Some are solitary, but others form in clusters. Some grow opposite from each other. Others alternate.

3 See what kind of textures your leaves have. Are they smooth and waxy, or coarse and rough? Do they have spiny parts or crinkled edges?

Compound

Lobed

OAK

VIRGINIA CREEPER

Linear

WILLOW

Varied color

MAPLE

Smooth

Spiny   HOLLY

BEECH

110 Track leaf colors

5 MINS

Leaves change color as they grow and age. Most start out bright green but turn many different shades before they die. Photograph the same plant leaf every month for a year to see how it changes.

Track the changes

111 Make leaf lanterns

20 MINS

Transform plain glass tealight holders—or even jam jars—into beautiful leaf lanterns. Simply stick on some pretty leaves, coat them with glue, and let the light shine through.

What you need
- Decorative leaves
- Craft glue and brush • Tealights
- Clear tealight holders or jars

1 Flatten your leaves by pressing them under heavy books overnight. Coat the outside of the glass with glue.

2 Press on your leaves in any pattern you choose. If it's fall, try to use red or gold leaves, but any design will be pretty when it's lit by candlelight.

3 Paint another thick coat of craft glue over the leaves. Let the leaves dry thoroughly, then ask an adult to drop in a tealight and light it for you. Lanterns are great if you're having an evening party. Just remember—never leave a lit candle unattended, and blow out the candle when you're finished.

112 Make shadow creatures

5 MINS

Shine a flashlight on a wall. See how many shadows of different creatures you can make with your hands, using them one at a time or together. Add sound effects if you like!

113 Make a chalk sidewalk picture

What you need
- Colored chalk
- Paving stones or patio

You don't always need paper to draw pictures. Use your patio or garden path as a palette and you can create colorful chalk artworks that will wash away with the next rain shower.

1 Choose a smooth section of patio in a place where you won't have people stepping on your work. Ask permission first, though, and make sure that the chalk will wash off.

2 Decide what you want to draw. You could make one drawing in one place, or make a path out of flowers, stars, or fish, or trace around your hands to make a handprint picture.

Use different colors to make contrasts

3 Make your drawing as complicated or as easy as you like. The choice is yours! Then stand back and admire your artwork.

114 Trace someone's shadow

Trace a friend's shadow. Mark where your friend stood, then come back in an hour to see where the shadow falls. Repeat to see how the outline changes. Does your friend get taller or shorter?

This shadow is getting smaller

115 Play backyard concentration

Test your nature identification skills with this game of concentration. Match pairs of images and you'll improve your observational skills as you play. Take photos and make cards from your own pictures.

What you need
- Wildlife and plant images
- Posterboard for backing
- Glue

1 Find pictures of plants and animals you see in your yard. Print two copies of each and glue them to posterboard. You need at least 10–12 different species.

2 Shuffle , then lay the cards face down. Each player takes a turn, revealing two cards. If they are a pair, the player keeps them. If not, the cards are turned over. The player with the most pairs wins.

3 Alternatively, take the cards outside and deal them. The first person to spot and name everything on their cards wins.

Pigeons can remember faces and will avoid people who shoo them away!

116 Dissect an owl pellet

Piece of pellet

Mouse or vole skull

Tiny mammal bones

Break the pellet into two or three pieces, then soak them in water for an hour to soften. Use tweezers to tease them apart and find out what the owl has eaten.

117 Plant a fairy ring

Fairy rings aren't all about toadstools and mushrooms. Plant a secret fairy ring at the bottom of your yard using ornamental grasses and tall, sweet-smelling flowers, and you can create your own magical place.

What you need
- 2 stakes • Long piece of string • Shovel
- Tape • Compost
- Tall, scented flowers
- Ornamental grasses

1 Push a stake into the grass and tie one end of the string to it. Tie the other end to the second stake. Use it to mark out the ring.

2 Dig a trench around the ring and add compost. Take each plant out of its pot, put it in the trench, and cover with soil.

3 Press down the soil and water the plants well. Hang lanterns, lights, or other decorations around the ring.

118 Make a garden lantern

Paint a jam jar with special glass paint, or use household paint and put a layer of varnish on top. When dry, wrap wire around the top of the jar so you can hang it. Put a tealight inside and ask an adult to light it for you.

Use different colors

Light shines through

119 Make a wind vane

A wind vane faces into the wind—not toward the direction it's going. Track changing wind patterns with this wind vane. Attach colored clothespins to make a compass and chart the exact wind direction.

What you need
- Letter-sized sheet of posterboard • Tape
- Scissors • 2 pennies
- Pen cap • Skewer
- Stake • 4 clothespins

1 Fold the posterboard in half lengthwise. Draw from the bottom corner to the top center fold and cut through both layers.

2 Tape the pennies inside near the tip. These will help to balance the vane when it's complete. Tape the vane shut.

3 Balance the vane on a pencil to find the balance point. Mark this point and tape the pen cap to it. Tape the skewer to the stake. Push it into the ground.

Pivot point

4 Use a compass to align the clothespins on the stake. Put the vane on the skewer and watch it spin.

Point red clothespin north

Each matches a compass point

120 Time thunder and lightning

When you see lightning flash, count the seconds until you hear thunder. Sound travels a mile every 5 seconds, or a kilometer every 3, so you can calculate how close the lighting strike was.

121 Identify types of trees

There are thousands of different trees in the world, but you can identify the ones in your yard by looking for "marker clues" like a detective. Note them down and consult a guide, and it will tell you what your tree is.

1 First, look at the leaves. Are they long, thin leaves or wider, flat leaves with veins? Trees with needlelike leaves are conifers—evergreens that keep their leaves all year round. Trees with broad, flatter leaves are deciduous—most lose their leaves in the fall.

2 Conifers like pines have sharp, needlelike leaves, but a cedar has flatter ones. The leaves of deciduous trees can have an alternating or opposite pattern, with one simple leaf or several small leaves on a single stem.

3 Look at the tree's bark—is it smooth or rough? Brown or silver? What about shape—is the tree tall and pointed or does it cast a wide, rounded shadow? Does it have fruit or cones?

BROAD

CONICAL

COLUMNAR

SPREADING

NARROW

GNARLED

122 Play a game of Pooh sticks

5 MINS

Take two sticks, tie grass to one to help identify it, and drop both into flowing water on one side of a bridge. Cross to the other side of the bridge and see which stick comes out first.

Watch the sticks pass by

123 Plant an egg carton

Many things we use for one purpose can also serve another. The carton that holds your eggs, for instance, is ideal for sowing plants in spring. Give your favorite vegetables a head start. Get planting!

What you need
- Egg cartons
- Seed compost
- Seeds
- Trowel
- Water

1 Tear off the lid. Fill the carton holes with seed compost. Sprinkle your seeds thinly on top. Cover with compost.

2 Water the seeds gently, then label them. Place the carton on a sunny windowsill. Keep the soil moist, but not wet.

Remove weaker seedlings

Transplant once enough leaves appear

3 When your seedlings sprout, thin out the weaker ones. Once their second set of leaves has formed, the seedlings are ready to transplant.

124 Use toilet-paper rolls as planters

Put toilet-paper roll tubes in a shallow tray; fill each with seed compost. Plant one seed per tube. Keep moist. When leaves appear, plant in the ground.

One seed per tube

Tubes break down when planted

125 Train honeybees

30 MINS

Honeybees are especially good at remembering where the best flowers are. When they find new ones, they tell their hive-mates by dancing. Test their memories with some fake flowers.

You will need
• Posterboard in five colors • Scissors
• Water • Cup • Sugar
• 5 bottle caps

1 Cut five different colored flowers out of posterboard. Mix sugar water in a cup. Put the flowers in the sun, with a bottle cap in the center of each.

Bees return to empty cap

3 Take away the sugar water. Bees will return to the same flower, remembering it by sight, even when the food isn't there.

2 Put sugar water in one bottle cap. The first bees will tell the hive about the food, and other bees will come to the same flower.

Ask an adult to remove the food—bees can sting you if they get angry.

126 Is it a bee or a wasp?

2 MINS

Bees are covered in fuzzy hairs and have short bodies. Wasps are smooth and streamlined, with a narrow waist dividing their thorax and abdomen (body parts).

Hair
Smooth thorax
Waist
Abdomen
BEE
WASP

127 Make a spider's web

Spider webs may feature in horror movies, but if you look at them closely, you'll find they're geometric works of art. Make one yourself and you'll really appreciate just what masters of construction spiders are.

What you need
• Square of thick cardboard • Small wire ring • Thumbtacks • Black yarn • White thread • Scissors

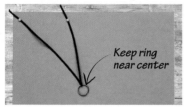

Keep ring near center

1 Cut six long lengths of yarn. Thread one strand through the ring and pin the ends to the edge. Trim off the excess.

2 Repeat until all the black radial strands are pinned in place and the ring hangs securely in the center of the square.

Tie or glue thread when you reach the center

3 Tie one end of the white thread to a side tack. Thread it around the other thumbtacks, looping around them as you go. Continue to the center in a spiral.

Loop the white thread around the black

128 Watch a spider make a dragline

Spiders use a dragline, a single strand of silk, to connect themselves to their webs or to steady themselves when jumping through the air. The next time you see a spider, see if you can spot its dragline.

This line holds the spider steady

129 Create an ice flower mobile

20 MINS

You can make cool biodegradable art that will add to the beauty of your yard—while the art lasts. Just freeze flower heads, leaves, and plant stems in ice and hang them to enjoy before the Sun comes out.

What you need
- Fancy ice-cube molds • Thread
- Scissors • Flower heads, leaves, twigs • Water

1 Arrange your flowers and plants in each ice-cube pocket. Cut a loop of thread to hang each cube.

2 Fill the tray, putting a thread loop in each pocket. Freeze the tray for a few hours, then hang your mobiles.

Conifer twig

Flower heads

Scalloped edge

130 Make an orange pomander

15 MINS

Get that Christmassy smell by making pomanders. Simply stud oranges or mandarins with cloves. Run your fingernail gently over the fruit's skin to release its fragrance.

Decorate with ribbon

131 Make a waterfall wall

40 MINS

Recycle plastic containers into this fantastic water wall. Put a bucket at the bottom to catch the water and keep reusing it. Ask an adult to help you drill holes for this project.

What you need
- Clean plastic bottles and containers
- Scissors or craft knife • Drill • Screws
- Wall or fence panel

1 Cut holes in the sides of the bottles. These must be large enough to catch the water and to get your hands inside to hold and attach the screws to the wall.

2 Cut a small X into the side, near the hole, then screw the container to the fence. Use two screws per bottle.

3 Tilt the bottles slightly as you attach them to the wall. Test the water flow. Put a bucket at the bottom and start the waterfall.

132 Make a waterslide

10 MINS

Lay some partially inflated air mattresses on the grass. Position the end of a garden hose on them, turn on the water, and let the sliding fun begin!

It's fun to run and slide!

133 Build a container pond

40 MINS

Ponds make great wildlife havens. Even if you only have a balcony, you have room for a mini pond. Put it in a shady spot so it won't dry out, and remember to place it in its final position before filling it with water.

What you need
- Clean bricks/gravel
- Container holding at least 10 gallons (40 liters)
- Aquatic plants
- Rainwater

1 Put the bricks in the container bottom to make a platform for the plants. Pour in the gravel. Fill two-thirds full with rainwater.

2 Add plants: oxygen-makers first, then edging plants. Leave the edging plants in pots, but add some gravel to weigh them down.

3 Fill the pond with rainwater. Put one or two floating plants on top. Add a stick bridge so any creatures that fall in can escape.

Stick reaches to edge

134 Let life begin

5 MINS

Fill a jar with rainwater. After a few days, does it turn green? This means you have microscopic life in your jar. Look closely—you may also see insect larvae swimming around.

135 Build a shelter

15 MINS

Shelters come in all shapes and sizes. One of the easiest types to make is a tent held up by one central line. Ask an adult to help you find a place in your yard where you can make one.

1 Decide where you want to locate your shelter. Find two points where you can attach the ends of your central line. A fence post or tree branch would work, or you could put a hook in the side of a shed.

2 Set up your line, making sure it's not so high off the ground that your tent won't reach. When you're happy with the height, lay your sheet or blanket over the line so that the sides are even.

3 Find something to keep the corners in place, such as bricks or stones. You can also tap small sticks into the ground and tie the corners to those. Crawl inside and enjoy!

Use your shelter as a hideout or clubhouse

136 Stack a stone tower

5 MINS

Collect a large number of flat stones of different sizes. Start with the largest ones and see how high you can stack them to make a stone tower.

Use smaller stones as the tower grows taller

137 Use leaves to make an owl mask

40 MINS

You can make marvelous things using what nature provides. Turn a handful of leaves and acorns into this fantastic owl mask. Collect different shapes and colors and see what kind of owl you can become!

What you need
• Leaves, acorns, and nutshells • Cardboard
• Pencil • Scissors
• Glue • Short stick or cane • Tape

1 Draw a mask shape on a piece of cardboard and cut it out. Make eye holes. Gather your different leaf shapes.

2 Lay the leaves and nutshells on the mask, glue them in place, and let dry. Tape a stick to one side so you can hold it up to your face.

Ferns and grasses

Nutshellls frame eyes

Thin leaves for feathers

138 Make a leaf crown

20 MINS

Cut a strip of cardboard long enough to fit around your head, with a 1½ in (4 cm) overlap. Glue leaves to the band. Tape the band ends together to make the crown.

Taller leaf in the center

Smaller leaves around sides

139 Collect runner bean seeds

15 MINS

Most plants produce seeds, ranging from tiny poppy seeds to enormous coconuts. Collect and store runner bean seeds properly, and you'll have plenty to plant next year.

What you need
- Scissors
- Brown paper envelopes
- Pencil
- Runner bean plants

1 Leave a few pods on the vine. When they start to dry out and split along the pod center, cut them off near the stem.

2 Open the pod. Remove all the beans, but discard any that are deformed or split. Let them dry out thoroughly.

Plant your collected seeds

3 Put them in a brown paper envelope. Store them in a dry, cool place until next year. Then start off new plants by putting one bean in a yogurt cup of soil.

> It's time to transplant your new bean plants when they have grown full leaves.

140 Dry beans for food

40 MINS

To dry beans for eating, use a needle to pull clean thread through the top third of each bean. String them about 1 in (2.5 cm) apart and hang in a warm, dry, dark place for 1–2 weeks. Store them in an airtight jar.

Dried beans

141 Measure space with your hands

Astronomers measure the size of stars and planets and the distance between them in degrees. You can use your hand to measure degrees—"measuring space" as you do so.

What you need
- Your hands
- A starry night

1 Start with your index fingertip. The width of this fingertip, held out at arm's length, is about 1 degree across.

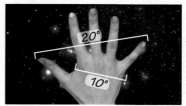

2 Now curve this finger and hold it side-on, still at arm's length. Starting at the top, your three finger joints are equal to roughly 3, 4, and 6 degrees wide.

3 Finally, use your entire hand. The measure from your pinky fingertip to your thumb is about 20 degrees, while the width of your palm is about 10 degrees.

142 Make a moonscape

15 MINS

Fill a baking sheet with sand. Smooth the sand with a ruler, then drop round objects into it. Try a grapefruit, a marble, a ball bearing, or a grape. Each represents a "meteor strike" on your moonscape.

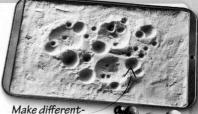

Make different-sized craters

143 Make a feather collection

Birds come in a variety of shapes and sizes. One of the most striking things about birds is their plumage. Some are brightly colored, others are drab. Discover the wonder of feathers for yourself by starting a collection.

What you need
• Feathers
• Field guide to birds

1 Try to find clean-looking, whole feathers. Discard any that are broken, have ragged edges, or have chunks missing from them.

2 Use a field guide to identify which species of bird a feather belongs to. Look for clues in terms of color, stripes, or speckles to help you match the feather to the bird.

3 Try to work out which part of the bird the feather comes from. Long, slender ones are likely to be tail feathers, while small ones with down at the base are body feathers.

Striped tail feather

Body feather

Central shaft

DUCK

GOOSE   PHEASANT   KESTREL   JAY

144 Unzip a feather

3 MINS

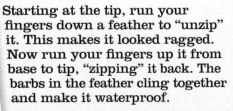

Starting at the tip, run your fingers down a feather to "unzip" it. This makes it looked ragged. Now run your fingers up it from base to tip, "zipping" it back. The barbs in the feather cling together and make it waterproof.

Barbs

145 Make lavender soap

40 MINS

Some garden plants can have all kinds of uses, including helping us to keep clean. Why not turn some fresh lavender flowers into this perfumed soap?

What you need
- Melt-and-pour soap base
- Plastic mold • Lavender
- Lavender oil • Knife
- Microwave-proof bowl
- Mortar and pestle

1 Take the heads off the lavender stalks and grind them into a fine powder with the mortar and pestle.

2 Microwave the soap in a bowl for 40 seconds. Stir in the lavender powder and oil.

Fresh lavender

3 Pour the mixture into the mold. Sprinkle whole lavender buds on top. Let it set overnight, then chop it into bars.

Whole lavender buds

146 Create a flower perfume

1 HR

Remove the petals and buds from one large rose and three lavender heads. Ask an adult to boil two cups of water in a pan, add the flowers, and simmer for 15 minutes. Let cool and strain into a container.

Rose petals

147 Make a leaf picture frame

Show off a drawing or photograph with a beautiful frame made from leaves and other plant materials gathered from your yard or a park. If you're in a park, only collect items that have fallen to the ground.

1 Place a photo or drawing on a sheet of cardboard and draw around it with a pencil. Use a ruler to draw a smaller rectangle inside. Make sure the edges are wide enough to hold the ornaments. Cut it out.

2 Arrange your items on the frame, then glue them in place and let dry. Glue the frame onto your picture, tape a piece of string on either side, and hang your creation for everyone to see!

Evergreen fronds

Glue your items in place

Nutshells in corners

148 Make a nature bug

Collect twigs, leaves, and nutshells. Make a body out of clay. Add twigs for legs and antennae and push shells into the body. Use leaves or winged seeds for wings, and berries or stones for eyes.

149 Make an erupting volcano

Volcanoes erupt in various ways. Some ooze lava slowly, but others hurl rocks and molten material sky-high. Make this model volcano and watch your very own Vesuvius erupt.

What you need
- Plastic bottle • Tray
- Water • Measuring cup
- Food coloring • Dishwashing liquid • Sand • Funnel
- Baking soda • Vinegar

1 Use the cup to measure how much water the bottle holds. Put the empty bottle on the tray.

2 Pile moist sand around the bottle, as above. Fill the cup with warm water equal to two-thirds of the bottle. Add two heaping tablespoons of soda and stir.

3 Add a spoonful each of food coloring and dishwashing liquid to the cup. Stir. Use the funnel to pour the cup's contents into the bottle. Add half a cup of vinegar to the measuring cup. Pour it into the bottle and stand back. The eruption is about to take place!

"Lava" flowing

It's best to do this outside!

150 Make a stone float

Pumice is a rock made from frothy lava. It contains lots of holes that make it lighter than other rocks. Drop a pumice stone in a bowl of water to see it float. It will sink eventually, as water enters the air holes.

Air holes

151 Build a wormery

1 HR

Earthworms are amazing tunnelers, creating rich compost as they go and adding oxygen and nutrients to the soil. Build this wormery and watch them at work.

What you need
• 3-sided frame, 12 x 8 x 2 in (30 x 20 x 5 cm)
• 2 clear plastic sheets
• 4 bulldog clips • Compost, soil, sand, leaves • Worms

1 Ask an adult to help you make the frame. Cut two sheets of clear plastic almost the same width as the wood.

3 Stand your wormery on a tray. Fill the gap with alternate layers of compost, sand, and soil. Lightly moisten the layers, then add the worms. Cover the top with leaves.

2 Glue the sheets to either side of the frame. Secure the ends with the bulldog clips. The clips also give the worm farm stability, so leave them in place.

4 Drape the wormery with a cloth and put it in a cool, dark place. After a few days, check to see how busy your little wrigglers have been!

152 Is it a head or a tail?

3 MINS

You can tell which end of a worm is which by finding its saddle—the thick band that forms in adult worms. A worm's head is near the saddle. With young worms you have to see which end moves forward.

Tail

Head

Saddle

153 Make conkers

Conkers is a children's game that has been played in Britain and Ireland for about 200 years. All you need to play are two players and some horse chestnuts.

What you need
- Horse chestnuts
- Distilled white vinegar
- Skewer or bradawl
- String or strong thread about 12 in (30 cm) long

1 Cover the chestnut with vinegar and soak it for two minutes. (Note: Have an adult help you with all these steps!)

2 Preheat the oven to 425°F (250°C). Bake the chestnuts for 1½ minutes. Use oven mitts to take them out, and let cool.

Chestnut in its shell

Knotted string

3 When the chestnuts are cool enough to handle, pierce each one. Pull the string through each one and tie a knot securely. Ready, set... play!

Be careful when playing conkers—pieces can fly off when the chestnuts break.

154 Play a game of conkers

Toss a coin to see who starts. Player one takes three strikes at player two's conker, then hangs his or her conker. Player two goes next. The winner breaks the other player's conker.

Hold the striking conker in your fingers

Hang the conker to be struck

155 Grow beans on a teepee

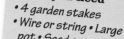
One of the easiest ways to grow runner beans in a small space is by training them up a pot-plant teepee. It's really easy to do, and you'll be amazed at the harvest your plants produce.

What you need
- 4 garden stakes
- Wire or string • Large pot • Seed compost
- Trowel • Bean seeds
- Watering can

1 Fill a large plant pot with seed compost. Insert four stakes into the soil, then tie the ends together in a teepee shape.

2 Make a small hole at the base of each stake with your finger. Plant one bean by each stake. Cover with soil and water well.

3 As your plants grow, guide their stems up the stakes. You may need to tie them in loosely with twine to start.

4 Soon your beans will climb up the stakes by themselves. Keep them watered well in dry weather—misting them helps, too!

156 Watch a plant climb

5 MINS

Many plants use tendrils to climb. Look at sweetpeas and you'll see thin, green "fingers" coiled tightly around whatever they touch. Watch how they do this over several days.

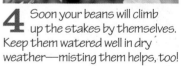

Curly tendril

Sweetpea flower

157 Make a hidden image

10 MINS

Want to hide an important map or keep a secret message safe from prying eyes? All you need is a lemon and source of heat to turn yourself into a special agent!

What you need
- Half a lemon • Water
- Bowl • Spoon
- Paintbrush
- White paper • Heat of the Sun or a lamp

1 Squeeze the juice from half a lemon into a bowl. Add several drops of water and use the spoon to mix them thoroughly.

2 Use the paintbrush to make a picture or write a message on the paper. Let it dry—the image should now be invisible.

3 When you want to see the image, hold it up in the hot sun, or next to a lightbulb if it's a cloudy or cold day. The heat from the light will reveal your picture.

Lemon juice turns brown when it's heated. Adding water makes it very hard to see at normal temperatures.

158 Reveal a secret message

5 MINS

Pick a dandelion and use the sap that oozes out of the stem to write a message on a piece of paper. You won't see the message while it's wet, but just watch what happens as it dries!

Dandelion sap turns brown when it dries

159 Race over an obstacle course

What you need
- Obstacles (plastic furniture, buckets, boxes)—anything you can go over, under, around, or through!

If you like running races, why not set up your own obstacle course? Use whatever you can find to create hurdles, tunnels, slaloms, and water obstacles. Then time yourself and your friends on the course.

1 Set up hurdles at different heights. Use a stake or a broomstick placed across two chairs for one, then make a lower one using buckets or boxes. Or simply lay a rope on the ground.

2 Make a zigzag slalom out of empty plastic bottles, flowerpots, boots, or stones.

3 For tunnels, crawl under a garden bench or the chair hurdle in step 1, or open both ends of a large cardboard box and go through that. Splash through a wading pool and make a step test from plastic hoops laid on the ground.

Lay a stake over two buckets for a low hurdle

160 Try skipping

Grab a jump rope and see how fast or how long you can jump rope. See if you can switch hands as the rope goes over your head, or jump on alternate feet.

Can you turn the rope twice between jumps?

161 Play limbo in your yard

45 MINS

Limbo began as a Caribbean dance contest. Today, it's a game of skill as players try to bend over backward while walking forward beneath a pole. How low can you go?

1 Push two poles 6 in (15 cm) into the ground about 4 ft (1.2 m) apart. Mark a point 3 in (7 cm) from the top of each.

2 Wrap wire around the marks, leaving a length to twist into a hook. These will hold the limbo pole.

3 Mark more spaces evenly down the length of each upright pole and add wire hooks to them all. Now you can start the game, moving the limbo pole lower and lower until you find a winner. If you like, put on some Caribbean music to accompany the game.

Don't fall!

162 Play a game of hoopla

10 MINS

Fill plastic bottles with colored water. Decide how many points each color is worth. Set them up with the highest points at the back, toss rings over them, and tally your score.

Try playing sitting or standing

163 Bury a time capsule

A time capsule is a collection of items you think would interest people (or yourself) in the future. You can write a letter to the future finder and include toys, coins, photos—anything you'd be happy to dig up yourself!

What you need
- Sturdy plastic box
- Items to bury—a letter, photos, toy, newspapers, etc.
- Parental permission!

1 Think about what you would like to learn about someone in 50–60 years' time—or longer. Write a letter about yourself.

2 Take a photo of yourself and your family and identify everyone on the back. Include their ages, too.

3 Add coins minted in the year the capsule is buried, as well as a newspaper listing current world events.

4 Put everything in a sturdy, weatherproof box, seal it, and bury it in the yard for future archeologists to find.

164 Make a map of your neighborhood

Draw a map of your area noting all the places of interest. Are there big buildings, such as a school or store? Is there a park or playground? Use a compass to help you position it all correctly.

165 Make a bird table

1 HR

Bird tables offer birds a safe place to eat, away from predators such as cats. You can birdwatch while they eat. Help an adult build your bird banquet table.

⚠️

What you need
• Weatherproof plywood cut into: tray: 12 in x 16 in x ¼ in (30 cm x 40 cm x 15 cm); tray rim: 5 ft x ½ in sq (1.5 m x 1 cm sq) cut into 2 x 16 in (40 cm) strips and 2 x 10 in (26 cm) strips; post-holder: 19 in x 1½ in sq (50 cm x 4 cm sq); post: 5 ft x 1½ in sq (1.5 m x 4 cm sq) • Screwdriver • 1 in (20 mm) nails • 2 in (55 mm) screws • Tape measure • Pencil • Saw • Hammer • Electric drill

1 Nail the four rim strips to the tray. Leave a gap at each end of the short strips to let rainwater escape. Cut the post-holder wood into four pieces.

Add food

Rainwater slot

3 Drill two holes through the post-holder. Fix screws to attach the post. Hammer the tray in the center to drive the post into the ground.

Position table in an open space

2 Screw the pieces to the tray, as shown. Saw one end of the post into a point. Push the square end into the post-holder.

166 Make a ground bird feeder

40 MINS

To make a ground bird feeder, make the tray and rim as in step 1 above. Nail or glue one piece of the post-holder to each tray corner to raise it off the ground. Add a wipeable liner, or pour the seed onto the wooden tray.

Seed on tray

Foot

167 Paint plant pots

Liven up your yard with some bright containers. Add acrylic paint to a terra-cotta pot and you can show off your plants as well as your artistic skills. Don't forget to weatherproof your designs with a layer of varnish.

What you need
- Terra-cotta pot
- Acrylic paint
- Glitter • Craft glue
- Paintbrushes
- Clear craft varnish

1 Paint the pot with a dark color toward the bottom. Use lighter shades of the same color as you move up the pot.

2 When the first coat is dry, add another color. Here we've put white paint daubs on a blue background to make clouds.

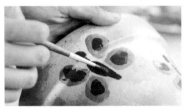

3 When this layer dries, add another. Paint flowers, bugs—anything you like. Paint a shape in glue and sprinkle with glitter. Varnish the pot when dry.

Flower design

168 Make a herb-lined pot

Cut flowers

Herbs tied on

Use string to tie herbs, such as rosemary, around the outside of a pot or basket. Fill the pot with flowers and give as a gift. Herbs stay fragrant for a long time.

169 Make a butterfly net

In spring and summer the air is filled with flying insects. To get a closer look, try catching some with this easy net. Simply wave it over plants and shrubs.

What you need
- 32 in (80 cm) square muslin
- Stapler • Wire hanger • Pliers
- 24 in (60 cm) stick
- 4 in (10 cm) flexible wire
- Strong tape

1 Fold over 2½ in (6 cm) on one edge of the muslin to make a hem for the hanger to go through. Staple it down along its length.

2 Cut off the hanger hook below the twist. Straighten the wire and slide it through the hem. Bend it into a circle, leaving two ends.

3 Staple together the sides and bottom of the net. Place the stick across the net and tie to the far side with wire. Tape the ends of the hanger to the stick.

170 Is it an insect or a spider?

Insects have six legs; spiders have eight. Insect bodies have three parts: head, thorax, and abdomen. A spider's body usually has two: a head and abdomen. Most insects have wings. Spiders have fanged jaws, but insects don't.

Eight legs

Six legs

INSECT

SPIDER

171 Go cloud-spotting

Just like people, clouds come in all shapes and sizes. Some are white and fluffy—like cotton balls. Others are gray and sheetlike. Go cloud-spotting and see how many cloud types you can identify.

What you need
- Your eyes
- Clouds
- Guide to cloud types

Cumulonimbus: large, tall thundercloud

Cirrus: high, wispy fibers

Cirrocumulus: high, small, fluffy

Cirrostratus: high, thin sheets

Altocumulus: mid-level, small, fluffy

Altostratus: mid-level, layered sheets

Stratocumulus: low, slightly fluffy sheets

Cumulus: low, fluffy, white or gray pillows

1 Start by looking at the cloud's shape. Is it puffy and round, spread out in a sheet, or wispy, like smoke? Is it hanging low in the sky or so high you can hardly see it?

172 Forecast the weather

5 MINS

A pinecone can act as a simple barometer. Set it on a shady windowsill. If the scales close, the humidity is high and it might rain. If it's open, the air is dry and the weather will be clear.

RAIN   FAIR

173 Shape an ivy man

Clipping plants into shapes is called topiary, and it can take years to do. But you can make a leafy figure by training fast-growing ivy on a wire frame. This ivy man should come to life in just months.

What you need
• Garden wire • Wire cutters • Container • Potting soil • Shovel made from twig and foil • 2 ivy plants

1 For the head, twist two lengths of wire into ovals, leaving enough extra to make the neck.

Add shovel for support

Clip ivy to keep shape

2 Twist wire into a body shape. Leave a spike on each foot to push into the soil. Attach the head and wrap the shape with more wire.

3 Fill the container with potting soil. Push the figure in place. Place an ivy plant at each foot and thread around the frame.

174 Train a plant

New growth

Covered shape

Plant pot

Make or buy a small topiary training frame. Put potting soil in a pot, plant a small-leafed plant, such as ivy or box, and put the frame over it. As the plant grows, keep wrapping new shoots around the frame and trim into shape.

175 Make a moth trap

Moths are beautiful and fascinating insects, but because they come out mainly after sunset, they can be hard to see. Moths are attracted to light, so make a moth catcher and get a close look at these night creatures.

What you need
- White sheet • String
- 2 flashlights • Stapler
- Cardboard box • Scissors
- 4 egg cartons (no lids)
- Double-sided tape

1 Hang the sheet on a piece of string or drape it over a wall. Hang a flashlight behind it, or point it at the front of the sheet.

2 Open the top box flaps and cut off the two short ones. Cut one of these into four strips. Tape the egg cartons to the walls.

3 Staple the strips to the box top so the two flaps make a valley with a narrow slit about 1 in (3 cm) wide in the center.

4 At sunset, put the box by the sheet and switch on the flashlights. Place one in the box. After an hour, check the trap.

176 Is it a butterfly or a moth?

Most moths come out at night; butterflies come out in the day. Moths spread their wings flat at rest; butterflies hold theirs upright.

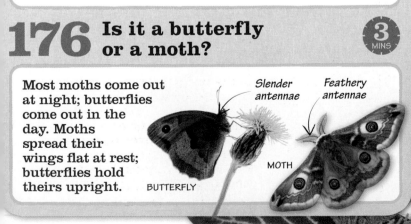

Slender antennae

Feathery antennae

BUTTERFLY

MOTH

177 Make a hanging star

Origami and kirigami are the Japanese arts of paper folding and paper cutting to make decorative objects. Use both of these art forms to make these magical paper stars and light up your backyard.

What you need
- Origami or other colored paper
- Pencil • Scissors
- Tape • Thin ribbon, for hanging

1 Fold the sheet of paper like an accordion. Make a shallow fold at the top, flip the paper, and bend an equal fold back on the first.

2 You should end up with a rectangle. Fold this in half, then make a diagonal 45-degree cut across one corner.

Make a star tree

Tape to join

3 Tape the edges of the first star points together. Unfold the star and tape the edges of the last two star points together. Tape ribbon to the back to hang it.

178 Spot shooting stars

Go out on a clear night. Spread a blanket on the ground so you can lie down and look up at the sky. If you see a sudden streak of light, you've probably spotted a shooting star.

179 Draw a treasure map

You don't need to be a pirate to own an ancient-looking treasure map. Age some paper with used tea bags, draw a trail to a treasure (real or imaginary), and you'll have a map that looks hundreds of years old!

What you need
- Pen • Paper
- Used tea bag
- Paper towels
- Cooking oil

1 First, draw the map on a piece of white paper. Include some identifiable landmarks, compass points, or add riddles and difficult or misleading clues to make the treasure harder to find.

2 When you're finished drawing, tear around the edges of the paper to make it look old—like a real ancient map.

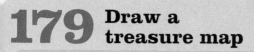

Aged paper

3 Lay the map out on paper towels and wipe it all over with a cold used tea bag. The paper will turn a light golden brown. Make sure it's really soaked through, then fold it up and let it dry overnight.

4 Carefully open the map. Wipe both sides with cooking oil, then pat it dry with paper towels and let the hunt begin!

180 Go on a treasure hunt

Hide some treasure in your yard—maybe a toy or a small box of trinkets. Draw a map to it, or hide clues in various places that lead to other clues. Ask friends to find the treasure.

Tie clues to trees

181 Dig a pond

Big or small, a pond is one of the best features you can put in a yard. It will attract new wildlife and give a boost to any already there. You don't even need a special pond kit—anything that holds water will do.

What you need
- Shovel • Waterproof container • Bricks or stones • Gravel
- Flat stones
- Water

1 Find a semi-shady spot. Mark out the pond's boundary on the ground with string. Dig a hole the same depth as the container.

2 Put the container in the hole—the top should be level with the ground. Fill in any gaps around it with soil.

3 Put bricks, rock, and gravel into the bottom to make levels. These will help any creatures that fall in to get out again, so make sure the levels reach the top.

4 Cover the edges with flat stones. Fill the pond with rainwater if you can. If you use tap water, let it settle a few days before adding plants.

182 Plant pond plants

20 MINS

Add plants to your pond to attract wildlife more quickly. You need four types: oxygenators to add air, deep-water plants, floaters, and edging plants. All help keep a pond healthy.

SWEET FLAG

WATER SOLDIER

BOG PRIMULA

183 Go on an orienteering event

If you like treasure hunts, you will love orienteering. The goal of this sport is to use specially drawn maps to find a sequence of flags or points on a set course in the fastest-possible time.

What you need
• Orienteering map
• Compass • Sneakers or walking shoes
• Comfortable clothes
• Waterproof jacket

1 Find a local orienteering activity near you and sign up for it. It may be a countryside course, but it could also be held in a park, in a town, or a city center.

2 Become familiar with orienteering maps. They usually use five colors to stand for different things:
• Black = tall buildings or cliffs
• Brown = landforms, such as gullies or hills
• Blue = water features
• Green = wooded areas
• Yellow = open areas

Find your way around the map's course

3 Practice using a compass. Orienteering maps are drawn using magnetic north, so learn how to find north on your compass.

184 Practice your geocaching skills

Take part in a real global treasure hunt. Players use GPS coordinates to lead them to "cached" (hidden) boxes of "treasure"—toys, badges, slips of paper— hidden in the countryside. See www.geocaching.com

185 Capture animal tracks in sand

20 MINS

When the Sun goes down, creatures that have hidden during the day start to become active. If you want to know what animals come into your garden or backyard at night, set up this easy "track trap" to find out.

What you need
- Sand
- Piece of wood
- Dog food
- Saucer or small, shallow dish

1 Cover an area of lawn with sand. Smooth it out with a piece of wood. The sand should be at least 1 in (2.5 cm) deep.

2 Put the dish of dog food in the center of the sand area, but be careful not to step on the sand or you'll have to smooth out the surface again.

3 The next morning, check for tracks. Take pictures or make drawings so you can identify what animal left them behind.

186 Identify animal tracks

10 MINS

You can figure out to what family your visitor belongs by counting the number of toes on the front and hind feet, and whether the claws are visible. The most common are cats, dogs, rodents, and mustelids.

FRONT   HIND
CAT

FRONT   HIND
DOG

FRONT   HIND
MUSTELID

FRONT   HIND
RODENT

187 Measure a tree's age

What you need
- Tape measure
- Large tree
- Pen and paper
- Calculator

Trees grow wider every year, as new wood is formed beneath the bark. This width, or "girth," is added at different rates for different species, but you can use an average for each type to find an approximate age.

This oak tree adds about ¾ in of girth each year

1 Identify the tree you want to measure. Measure around its trunk with a tape measure about 4½ ft (1.3 m) above the ground. Note the measurement.

2 Once you know the type of tree and its girth, use average growth rates to figure out its approximate age. Divide the girth by the growth rate.

3 The typical annual growth rates of some common trees are: oak—¾ in (1.5 cm); Douglas fir—3 in (7 cm); Scotch pine—½ in (1 cm); sycamore—1 in (2.5 cm).

188 Read some weather rings

15 MINS

The width of tree rings tells you what the weather was like in times past. Narrow rings show a lack of water. Wider ones are the result of good growing conditions.

Narrow = drought

Wide = good

GROWTH RINGS

189 Play hopscotch

Hopscotch has been played for centuries, so it must be fun! Play it alone or with friends. Either way, it will test your jumping skills. Only one foot goes in one square—or else you lose your turn!

1 Number 10 squares on the sidewalk (ask permission first). Square 1 stands alone, but arrange the rest as you like. Throw the marker into square 1.

2 Hop over square 1 to start. If two squares are side by side, one foot can land in each. Hop your way through all 10.

3 Turn around and hop back through the squares, picking up the marker in square 1 before you hop over it. Throw the marker into square 2 and start again.

190 Have a game of leapfrog

Get a friend to bend over or kneel on the ground. Jump over, pushing off on your friend's back as you go. Repeat until you run out of room—or breath!

Leap like a frog

191 Make a rain gauge

30 MINS

Meteorologists study weather in many ways. One method is by using a rain gauge to see how much rain has fallen. You can chart rainfall in your area by making this simple rain gauge.

What you need
- Clean plastic bottle • Scissors
- Measuring cup
- Permanent marker
- Ruler

1 Cut the top third off the bottle. Measure out 100 ml of water and pour it into the bottle. Mark this on the side of the gauge.

2 Mark your gauge up to 500 ml. Dig a shallow hole in the ground to put your gauge in so it won't blow away.

3 Whenever it rains, record how much has fallen each day on a chart. After five days, you should have a clear pattern of the rainfall levels in your area.

192 Splash in puddles

10 MINS

The next time it rains, put on your rain boots and go outdoors. Find as many puddles as you can and jump in them to see which one makes the biggest splash.

Have fun!

193 Make some fun planters

You don't need fancy pots to sow seeds. Make these planters from newspaper and you can start your seeds off indoors while the weather's cold. When it's warm enough, put them in the ground, pots and all!

1 Fold one edge twice to make a rim. Roll the paper into a tube, tucking one edge under the rim as you do so to hold it at the top.

2 Fold the bottom of the paper inward to make a base. Use the glass to flatten the base inside so that the tube stands up.

3 Fill the pots with compost, plant your seeds, and water lightly. Once the plants are big enough, put the pots into the soil. The paper will rot away.

194 Use juice cartons as planters

Cut the tops off clean, colorful juice cartons. Fill them with compost, then sow seeds for plants such as cut-and-come-again lettuces or herbs that won't need to be transplanted.

Juice carton

195 Create a woodland terrarium

30 MINS

Woodland trees provide food and shelter for squirrels and deer, but the leaves they lose are home to millions of tiny creatures, such as beetles, spiders, and centipedes. Build a terrarium to find out what lives in your local leaf litter.

What you need
- Trowel • 3 plastic bags • Old aquarium
- Small, shallow bowl
- Spray bottle
- Magnifying glass

1 Use the trowel to put dry and moist leaf litter in one plastic bag. Put soil from other places in the second bag, and bark, small branches, and cones in the third.

2 Spread soil on the aquarium floor and put a half-full bowl of water in one corner. Add leaf litter, branches, cones, and bark. Spray with water, then secure the lid in place.

3 Put the terrarium somewhere cool and shady. Spray it every day and top off the water dish. Feed any snails with lettuce leaves. Use the magnifying glass to spot animals. Once you've finished studying the creatures, take them back to where you found them and let them go.

Leaf litter

Soil layer

Water dish

196 Follow an ant trail

5 MINS

Find a nest or put some honey on the ground. Once the ants form a trail, put a leaf across their path. See how long it takes them to go around it.

Leaf "roadblock"

Ant trail

197 Play pebble dominoes

What you need
• 28 flat oval pebbles
• White paint • Guide to domino game pieces (from the internet) • A friend

Make a domino set with pebbles and white paint. Each domino should have a number from zero to six at each end. Paint on all the combinations (6/6, 6/5, 6/4, etc.) to make 28 dominoes in total.

1 Paint the pebbles and let them dry. Put the dominoes face down and mix them up. Have each player draw seven; keep the domino faces hidden.

2 Whoever has the double-six or the next highest double starts. The next player's domino must have a number to match an open end of the first. If you don't have a matching tile, you skip a turn.

3 Put the tiles end to end to show they match. Once two ends are together, no other tiles can be added to them. Take turns adding dominoes. If you play all seven of your tiles, you win!

198 Make a glow-in-the-dark snake

30 MINS

Collect one large pebble and a lot of smaller ones. Paint them with glow-in-the-dark paint, or decorate them with glow stickers. Set up your snake with the largest pebble for a head and the rest of the stones for its body. Wait until dark!

199 Make a bubble snake

Blowing one bubble is fun, but blowing a whole stream of them at once is better still. Blow a bubble as long as your longest breath, and see how long a bubble snake you can make with this bubble blower.

What you need
- Clean plastic bottle
- Scissors • Rubber band
- A dishcloth
- Plastic bowl
- Dishwashing liquid

1 Cut off the bottom of the plastic bottle with scissors. Cut the the dishcloth into a circle just larger than the bottle opening.

2 Put the dishcloth over the opening and secure it in place with a rubber band.

Blow as long as you can!

3 Mix two parts dishwashing liquid to one part water in a shallow bowl. Dip the cloth end of the blower into the bowl, put your mouth to the other end, and blow.

200 Make a water painting

5 MINS

Take a container of water and sit down on the sidewalk or on a patio. Use either your fingers or a paintbrush to "paint" pictures of whatever you like on the dry surface.

Fingerpaint with water

201 Make a toadstool ring

40 MINS

Turn plastic eggs and craft sticks into magical toadstools. Painting them is a great activity for a rainy day. Make lots of them and you'll be able to set up your toadstool ring outside when the Sun is shining.

What you need
- Plastic eggs
- Foil • Egg carton
- Craft sticks
- Acrylic craft paint
- Paintbrushes

1 Put half an egg into a long piece of foil. Mold the foil around the outside of the egg top to make your toadstool cap.

2 Push a stick inside the foil and cap. Scrunch the foil to hold the stick in place. Wrap the remaining foil around the stem.

3 Paint the toadstool cap one color. Set it in an egg carton to dry, then paint spots in another color. When dry, push the stems into the ground to make a ring.

202 What's eating your leaf?

2 MINS

Plant-eating insects leave tell-tale holes in leaves. Weevils cut notches around the edges, while slugs and earwigs make holes in the middle. Leaf miners chew tunnels. Check a bug guide for information.

Damage caused by a leaf miner

203 Make lemonade

Summer isn't complete without cool, refreshing lemonade. You can make your own—it's easy and quick to do. Use limes instead of lemons, if you prefer.

What you need
- 4 lemons • Wooden spoon
- 2 cups water
- ½ cup granulated sugar

1 Squeeze the juice from all the lemons. Pour the juice into a large container.

2 Add the water and stir the liquids well, using a wooden spoon.

3 Add the sugar and stir well until all the sugar dissolves. Put the lemonade in the refrigerator to chill.

4 Pour it into a glass filled with ice cubes, or pour it into a small soda bottle. Serve with a bendable straw.

Add a slice to make it extra tangy!

204 Make lemonade ice-pop treats

Ice-pop treat

Use up leftover lemonade by making ice pops. Unwrap and place some lollipops—such as fizzy or fruity ones—in an ice-cube tray. Pour in lemonade and freeze until set.

205 Make an earwig hide

Fast-moving earwigs belong to a group of bug that is "thigmotactic," meaning they prefer small, cramped spaces like cracks or crevices. This can make them hard to catch, but making this hide should do the trick.

What you need
- Plastic flowerpot
- Short bamboo stake
- Honey
- Straw

1 Block up any holes in the flowerpot and stuff the pot loosely with straw. Drizzle a little honey over the straw.

2 Push a short stake into the ground near a compost heap or flowerbed. Position the upturned flowerpot on top of the stake.

3 Check the hide after about a week. There should now be several earwigs inside, and you'll be able to get a good look at them without losing them down a small space. Just let them go when you're finished.

Males have curved pincers

206 Tempt earwigs with food

You can tempt earwigs with a variety of foods. They like rotting plant matter, food scraps, and fungi, but they like sweet things as well. Try different foods to see which works best.

207 Identify wader bill shapes

What you need
- Binoculars
- A guide to wader bill shapes (see below)

The next time you're at the beach, look at the birds walking and feeding along the shoreline. These are waders, and they have some of the most amazing bills. See which ones you can spot.

1 Waders' bills come in many lengths and shapes, to allow their owners to feed on different foods. What kinds can you see?

2 Long, curved bills let birds probe deep in the sand for lugworms. Oystercatchers use theirs to prize open mussel shells.

3 Short-billed waders like plovers and sandpipers feed on snails and clams that live closer to the surface.

Some waders wash their food before swallowing it, so you can see exactly what it's eating.

Oystercatcher

Curlew

Turnstone

Plover

Godwit

Sandpiper

208 Sift a mudflat sample

Mudflats can be tricky places, so take care when collecting a sample. Push the mud through a strainer. Mud snails, lugworms, tiny clams, and small worms should appear.

Mudflat sample

Fine mesh

Brush to push mud through

209 Make a wheat doll

Wheat dolls of all kinds of designs were made in ancient times from the last sheaf of wheat cut at harvest. You can make this simple one to hang in your kitchen.

What you need
- Wheat stalks or straw
- Scissors
- String, raffia, or thread
- Leaves

1 Grab a handful of stalks and tie them in the middle to make a waist. Divide one end into two legs. Tie each at the knees and ankles.

2 Divide the upper half into three. Make two arms in the same way as the legs. Fold and tie the last bunch to make the head.

3 Wrap straw around the middle to fill out the body and tie it in. You're now ready to add some leaf "clothes" if you like.

4 Position the leaves as you want them, then use straw or raffia to tie them to the figure. Add a hat if you choose.

210 Make a corn husk doll

25 MINS

Corn husks have long been used to make harvest figures. Peel the husks off the corncobs and let them dry, then tie the husks into arms, legs, and a head. You can paint on a face, or add felt "buckskin" clothes for a Native American feel.

Add a "leather" fringe

211 Make your own bowling game

20 MINS

What you need

- 10 small plastic soda bottles, all the same size
- Food coloring
- Water • Tennis ball

You don't need a special alley to bowl. Just recycle some plastic bottles, set them up, and use a tennis ball as a bowling ball. Keep track of the scores and see who's the best bowler you know!

Try over- and underarm bowling

Add decorations on top—these are worth more points

1 Wash the bottles and remove all labels. Put a few drops of food coloring in each, then fill them up with water. Screw on the lids—make sure they're closed good and tight.

2 Add decorations on the sides or tops, if you want— you can make these worth more to knock down if you like.

3 Set up your bowling pins on level ground in a triangle shape—start with a row of 1, then 2, 3, and 4. Grab your tennis ball (or any small ball) and start bowling!

212 Play glow-in-the-dark bowling

30 MINS

Put a glow stick in each of 10 clear plastic bottles. Fill the bottles with water and screw the lids on tight. Arrange them in a triangle. Bowl with a soccer ball if the bottles are large. *Activate them first!*

213 Grow your own stalactites

20 MINS

Stalactites form when minerals dissolved in water are left behind as the water drips from the moist ceilings of caves. With this simple project, you can grow your own in just a few days.

What you need
- 2 glass jars • Shallow dish
- Spoon • 2 paper clips
- Hot tap water • Pitcher
- 3 ft (1 m) length of yarn
- Baking soda

1 Set the jars on either side of the dish. Fold the strand of yarn in half, then fold it in half again. Twist it tightly.

2 Attach a paper clip to each end of the yarn. Put one end in each jar. Move the jars close enough to make a dip in the yarn.

3 Add baking soda to a pitcherful of hot tap water until no more dissolves. This makes a concentrated solution.

4 Pour the solution into both jars, and keep any leftovers to top off as needed. Stalactite crystals will appear in 2–3 days.

Solution drips into dish

Stalactite

Stalagmite

214 Tell stalactites from stalagmites

3 MINS

Stalactites hang from the top of caves, while stalagmites form on cave floors. To remember the difference, think of the "c" in stalactite standing for "ceiling" and the "g" in stalagmite standing for "ground."

Stalagmites reach up

215 Trap insects in amber

40 MINS

Amber is the fossilized resin of extinct conifers. It often contains the bodies of ancient insects, trapped there thousands of years ago. You can make your own "amber fossil" of an insect overnight.

Pebble makes a natural shape

1 Look for dead insects on windowsills indoors or in spider webs outdoors. Press the pebble into the clay. Coat the mold with a little petroleum jelly.

What you need
- Dead insects • Pebble
- Modeling clay
- Clear modeling resin
- Yellow food coloring
- Toothpick
- Petroleum jelly

2 Ask an adult to mix the resin—a hardener is usually called for; make sure to follow instructions.

Ants are often found in amber

3 Add a drop of yellow food coloring to the resin, mix well, and pour into the mold. Drop a dead insect on top and push it gently into the resin with the toothpick. When the resin is dry, wash it in soapy water.

The insect will be preserved for years

216 Make amber jewelry

20 MINS

Make your amber fossils into necklaces, pendants, or keyrings. Ask an adult to drill a hole in one end so you can attach a chain. Otherwise, use a jewelry fitting such as a bell cap or bail for a really professional look.

Amber makes a great necklace

217 Make a garden plant label

40 MINS

It can be hard to tell which plant is which. Creating labels can help, and you can make your labels a lot more fun than just a name on a stick. Here are ideas for fantastic labels. Don't forget to add the plant names!

What you need
- Wooden skewer • Yogurt cups, plastic cartons and spoons, buttons, CDs • Waterproof glue
- Markers • Scissors

1 For a flower, cut out petals from plastic milk cartons. Glue them to the back of a CD, overlapping slightly as you go.

2 Glue a button in the center of each petal, and attach a pipe-cleaner center. Glue the flower to a wooden skewer.

3 Use markers to draw faces on spoons. Glue on pipe-cleaner hair and clothes cut from plastic cartons.

4 For bug labels, cut wings out of a milk carton and glue to a yogurt cup. Add a cork head and pipe-cleaner legs and feelers.

Plastic petals

Plastic wings

Pipe-cleaner center

Button

218 Make glow-in-the-dark characters

30 MINS

Collect smooth pebbles. Glue string legs and googly eyes to the pebbles. Decorate the bodies with glow-in-the-dark glue or stickers. When dry, turn out the lights and watch your creatures glow.

String legs

Glow glue

Googly eyes

219 Make a peashooter

A peashooter doesn't just shoot peas—it fires any small object into the air. Make this one to shoot beads, balls of foil, or paper. Better still, make two and see who can shoot the farthest!

What you need
- Small plastic container • Balloon
- Scissors • "Peas": beads, paper balls, or real dried peas

1 Cut the bottom off a small plastic container. Drink yogurt bottles are ideal—leave on the ridged neck.

2 Stretch a balloon over the ridged neck of the plastic container. Make sure it's a good, tight fit.

3 Put a "pea" in the cup end. Let it fall into the balloon. Grab the balloon and stretch it back. Aiming it away from people, let go and watch the pea fly!

Add decorations

220 Blow a grass trumpet

Pick a clean-looking blade of grass—the wider, the better—and hold it side-on between your thumbs so that it's taut. Blow between your thumbs. The grass vibrates to make a trumpet sound.

Blow in here!

221 Climb a tree

30 MINS

Climb a tree and you enter another world high off the ground where everything below looks smaller. From here you can see tree-dwelling animals at close range—or just have the best hiding place ever.

1 Find a big sturdy tree with healthy branches large enough to take your weight. Stretch up to reach the first branch. Grasp it firmly, then pull yourself up the trunk. Look for footholds in the form of bulges, crevices, knotholes, or smaller branches.

2 Once you've reached a big limb to stand on, make your way up the tree, keeping close to the trunk. Never move to another branch without a firm handhold. Avoid weak-looking or rotten branches, and try not to damage healthy ones as you climb. When you're done, climb back down the way you came.

Don't climb trees where birds and squirrels are nesting.

222 Play hide and seek

1 HR

Get at least two players. Choose someone to be "It" and a place for "home." "It" covers his or her eyes and counts to 10 as the players hide. "It" then tries to spot or catch the others before they reach home.

No peeking allowed!

223 Make a paper airplane

Making and flying paper airplanes is lots of fun, either on your own or with a friend. Once you've mastered making the basic plane shape, add tail flaps so you can turn your plane to the left or right.

What you need
- Letter-sized sheet of paper

1 First, fold the sheet of paper in half lengthwise. Open it back up and fold each top corner into the center to make a triangle.

2 Fold each corner over toward the center again. Make sure the bottom edges are as even as possible.

3 Fold the plane in half along the center line, then fold each wing down, one at a time. You should end up with a dart-shaped plane. See whose plane can fly the farthest!

224 Make a paper helicopter

Take a small square of paper and draw a cross about 1 in (2.5 cm) wide across the middle of it. Make diagonal cuts from the corners to the cross. Fold the same edges up and down on each arm. Make a small hole in the center and insert a short length of a drink straw. Let your helicopter fly!

225 Make flower print paper

You don't always need brushes to paint pictures. Collect different kinds of flowers and dip them in paint, then use these natural "paintbrushes" to make flower prints.

What you need
• Flowers • Paper sheets • Poster paint or watercolors
• Small plastic dishes or an artist's palette

Flowers

1 Choose the colors you want and pour a different color of paint into each dish or section of the artist's palette.

2 Pick a flower head. Dip it into one color and press it on a sheet of paper. Try different pressures to see what works best.

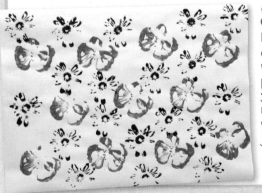

3 Dip another, different flower head in a different color to make a pattern with the first flower prints. Once dry, use your printed paper to make greeting cards or wrapping paper—or just frame it as it is!

226 Paint a flower with your hands

Paint your palm with poster paint. Press it on a piece of paper in a circle, like petals of a flower. Try another color with your other hand.

Press firmly for a good print

227 Lay a stick trail

20 MINS

Tracking is a great skill, and it's easy if you use stick symbols. Grab some friends and head for a nearby park or woodland. Lay a stick trail and see if your friends can find you.

What you need
- Sticks
- 2 watches
- A group of friends
- Let parents know where you're going

1 Agree on your symbols (see the activity below for ideas). Split into two teams—trailblazers and trackers. Be sure each member is with at least one other person and that each team has a watch.

2 Trailblazers should run ahead and lay the trail, using plenty of arrows, especially where the route is overgrown or several paths meet. They should then lie in wait for the trackers.

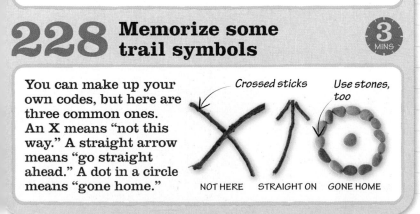

Stick symbol

3 After 10 minutes, it's time for the trackers to set off after the trailblazers. Time how long it takes for them to find where the trailblazers are hidden.

4 Once the the trailblazers have been found, swap roles and start again to see who's the best at each skill.

228 Memorize some trail symbols

3 MINS

You can make up your own codes, but here are three common ones. An X means "not this way." A straight arrow means "go straight ahead." A dot in a circle means "gone home."

Crossed sticks

Use stones, too

NOT HERE   STRAIGHT ON   GONE HOME

229 Test a plant's senses

Plants don't have eyes, but they know where the Sun is. Their stems move as they grow toward sunlight, which they need to make food. Put a plant in a box and see how it twists and turns.

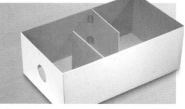

Shoot emerges

1 Cut out two cardboard rectangles, each as deep as the box and two-thirds as wide. Tape them to the box. Cut a small hole in one end of the box.

2 Paint the inside of the box black. Plant the bean in the pot, stand it in the box (with the hole at the top), and close the lid.

3 Remove the lid every day to see what's happening. The plant will slowly grow around the flaps until it finds the light.

230 Track a sunflower's movement

Plant a sunflower. Note the position of the flower head during the day as it turns from east to west. Plants that follow the Sun are called heliotropes.

Head tracks the Sun

Center contains seeds

231 Take a bark rubbing

Different trees have different types of bark. Some are smooth, some are rough, and some are in between, but all protect trees from injury and disease. Take rubbings to compare the bark of trees in your yard.

What you need
- Crayons
- Thick drawing paper
- Tape
- Field guide to trees (optional)

1 Choose a tree and brush off any loose particles from its bark. Tape a piece of paper to the tree trunk.

2 Rub the paper with the side of the crayon. This will show any unique notches, ridges, and other patterns in the bark.

Bark patterns

3 Remove the rubbing carefully from the trunk. Use a guide to identify the tree and write down its name, bark type, and color.

Crayons

232 Count tree rings

Find a tree's age by counting its growth rings—the light and dark circles shown in a cross-section of a trunk. One light plus one dark ring equals one full year of growth.

Light wood shows spring growth

233 Have a picnic

Having fun outdoors isn't always about doing things. Being outside makes everyday things special. A picnic, for instance, seems more fun than just plain lunch—so round up your friends and have one!

What you need
- Food, drinks, and snacks • Paper plates, napkins, and plastic cups
- Blanket • Friends

1 Invite some friends to your house, or arrange to meet them in a park (tell an adult where you intend to go). Ask each friend to bring one or two favorite picnic foods with them to add to the fun.

2 Think about what you'd like to eat. Do you want sandwiches or wraps? Cold cuts or sausages? Fruit and salad? Ask an adult to help you decide what would be nice for a sunny-day treat.

3 Spread the picnic blanket onto the ground. If the grass is damp, put plastic sheeting underneath it first.

4 After everyone arrives, set out your food and beverages, pass out plates, and enjoy your picnic! Don't forget to take all your garbage home.

234 Pass oranges without using your hands

Tuck an orange under your chin—it may take a few tries until you can hold it there. Then pass it among your friends without anyone using their hands.

Hold the orange with your chin

235 Make a rock pool viewer

40 MINS

Rock pools are fascinating places to explore. Ask an adult to help you make this rock pool viewer, and you'll get a clear look at the creatures in the pools without disturbing them.

1 Cut a piece of plastic tubing about 4 in (10 cm) long. Trace around one end on a piece of clear plastic.

2 Cut out the plastic circle with the scissors. Sand the edges of the tube. Glue the piece of plastic to one end of the tube.

3 Once the glue has dried, you're ready to use your viewer. Just push the plastic end into the water—and view.

> Take care when visiting rock pools—wet rocks and seaweed can be very slippery. Also watch out for high tide.

236 Go rock pooling

30 MINS

Find a pool. Either wade into it (in waterproof shoes), or watch from the sides. Keep still and wait— the wildlife will soon start to reveal itself. Look for fish, crabs, and shrimp.

Treat rock pool animals gently

237 Take a quadrat survey

Like animals, plants compete with each other to thrive. Use this quadrat regularly to keep a check on which plants win the battle for survival.

What you need
- 4 equal-sized pieces of wood, with an overlap
- Screws • Screwdriver
- Thumbtacks • Graph paper
- String • Ruler • Pencil

1 Ask an adult to help you screw the pieces of wood together to make a square frame. Use the ruler and pencil to mark each side into quarters.

2 Stretch string over the frame at the marks and fix with thumbtacks. Make 16 equal-sized squares.

3 Choose a spot for your quadrat. Use the graph paper to record the plants in each quadrat square, making a quadrat map.

Plant to record

Quadrat

Patch of soil

238 Take a transect survey

Tie a long piece of string to two poles. Drive one into the ground, pull the string tight, then push in the other pole. Record the position and height of all the plants along the string on graph paper.

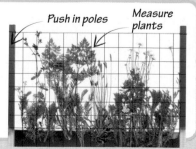

Push in poles

Measure plants

239 Start a worm poop factory

40 MINS

Worms are expert compost makers, turning plant matter into soil through their poop. Set up a poop factory and turn vegetable peelings into rich compost.

1 Ask an adult to cut out the bottom of one tub, leaving enough edge to hold a sheet of mesh. Put holes in the lid for air.

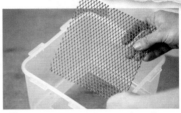

2 Cut the mesh to make a base. Add a layer of shredded paper, then sprinkle with water. Use compost for bedding.

3 Add worms to the compost and lightly cover with more compost. Place peelings in the mix and moisten with water. Stack on top of the other tub.

4 Cover with the lid and place in the shade. When poops drop through the mesh, remove them and put on the garden. Add fresh bedding and start again.

240 Be a worm charmer

5 MINS

Worms can feel vibrations. If you tap the ground very fast you can trick them into thinking it's raining. They'll come up to keep from drowning.

Tap very fast

Worms hate too much water

241 Plant a fruit tree

45 MINS

Every wildlife-friendly yard needs a tree. A tree's leaves provide shelter for many creatures, while birds and small mammals may nest in its branches. Here's how to plant a tree in your yard.

You will need
- Small tree, such as a crab apple • Shovel
- Watering can
- Rubber tree-tie
- Stake

1 Water the tree while it's still in the pot. Dig a hole twice as wide as the root ball and place the tree, still in the pot, in the hole.

2 Lay a stick across to check that the levels match. Remove the pot. Cover the roots with soil. Hammer in the stake at an angle, and tie it to the tree.

3 Water the tree regularly throughout its first year. Remove the stake when it is strong enough to stand by itself.

242 Grow an oak tree

30 MINS

Put some acorns and damp sawdust in a sealed plastic bag in the refrigerator until roots appear. Plant an acorn 2–4 in (5–10 cm) deep in a pot. Once it's 4 in (10 cm) tall, plant it outdoors.

Oak leaf

Acorn in cap

243 Make a flower change color

⏱ 1 HR

A cut flower uses vessels in its stem to draw water as moisture evaporates from its leaves and head. This experiment shows how this works—and lets you change a flower's color, too! ⚠

What you need
• 2 glasses • Spoon
• Food coloring
• Water • Tape
• White carnation
• Craft knife

Whole stem

Leaves lose moisture

Tape holds split stem

1 Ask an adult to help. Put the flower on a cutting surface. Slice its stem in two, from the base to halfway up.

2 Tape around the stem just above the top of the cut to prevent splitting. Fill both glasses three-quarters full of water. Add food coloring to one glass; stir well.

3 Put each half-stem into a glass and lean the flower against a window for support. The flower should start to change color after half an hour.

244 Arrange flowers in a jam jar

⏱ 15 MINS

Flower stems

Pick some flowers and arrange them in a bunch, then put a rubber band around the stems to keep them in place. Fill a jam jar with water and add the flowers. Make several jars and use them together as a centerpiece.

245 Detect small mammals

Many small mammals, such as mice and voles, live secretively in your yard, hiding from predators and humans. You may never spot them, but you can see where they've been!

What you need
- White letter paper • Scissors
- Wax paper • Stapler
- Nontoxic poster paint • Stick
- 12 in x 3 in (30 cm x 7 cm) plastic tube • Peanut butter

1 Cut two 3 x 1½ in (7 x 4 cm) pieces of wax paper. Staple one piece to each end of a strip of white paper.

2 Mix the paint with an equal amount of oil and brush it on both wax-paper strips. Slide the paper lengthwise into the tube.

3 Put peanut butter on the roof of the tube using the stick. Leave the tube out overnight, then check for footprints the next day.

Mouse prints

246 Trace tracks in the sand

When visiting the beach, look for prints in the sand. You may find some small mammal tracks, as well as those made by birds and other creatures.

Gull tracks

247 Make a lavender buddy

40 MINS

Hang bunches of lavender up to dry, and after a month you can use the flowers to make a buddy. He may look a little odd, but he'll keep your clothes smelling sweet!

What you need
- Old sock • Uncooked rice
- Dried lavender flowers
- Stick-on eyes • Fabric scraps • Sewing needle and thread • Pipe cleaners

1 Mix rice with the lavender and fill the sock, twist the end, and sew it closed. Sew on a mouth. Glue the eyes in place.

2 Fold over a scrap of fabric and draw some arms and legs. Cut them out and sew the raw edges together.

3 Sew the arms and legs to the body. Make "hair" by sewing pipe cleaners to your buddy's head and bending them into a wacky hairstyle.

248 Hang lavender bag bunting

1 HR

Cut two identical fabric shapes, fill with lavender, and sew them shut. Hang a line of them to keep a room smelling fresh.

Use clothespins for hanging

249 Create a desert garden

Not all gardens grow vegetables and flowers. You can make a pretty desert garden filled with succulents—plants that store water in thick, fleshy leaves and stems. Best of all—they won't prick you like cacti!

What you need
- Trowel • Spoon
- Shallow container
- Gravel • Soil-based potting compost
- Grit • Desert plants

1 Make sure the container has drainage holes in the bottom. Add a thin layer of gravel, then half-fill it with potting compost.

2 Carefully remove the plants from their pots. Plant them, filling in any gaps between the plants with more compost.

Leaves feel waxy

3 Lightly water the plants. Spoon the grit on top of the soil. This helps water drain away from the surface and prevents rot. It also gives a "desert look."

250 Look for lichens

Lichens are actually an alga and a fungus that live together in places with no soil. Look for their crusty or stringlike shapes on walls, trees, buildings, and rocks.

251 Make a windsock

A windsock is used to track which way the wind blows. Make this easy windsock and hang it in your backyard. Remember, the opening of the sock points into the wind.

What you need
- Fabric • Needle and thread • Thick and thin 30 in (76 cm) long ribbons • Scissors • String • Garden wire

1 Cut a 24 x 10 in (60 x 25 cm) piece of fabric. Hem the short sides. Fold and sew the edge of one long side to feed wire through.

2 Stitch wide and narrow ribbons to the unhemmed long side all along its length.

Windsock droops in slower winds

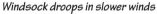

3 Push wire through the long hem. Bend the wire into a circle, twist the ends to join, sew the windsock sides together, then sew on string to hang.

252 Test which way the wind blows

If you can't see a weather vane, here is an easy way to find the wind's direction. Pick up something light, such as a few fallen leaves or blades of grass. Toss them into the air and see which way they go. Do it again to make sure.

253 Make a cloud in a jar

Three things make clouds—moist, warm air; coolness; and tiny particles in the air that make water vapor condense. This experiment uses hairspray to provide these particles.

What you need
- Jar with lid
- Aerosol hairspray
- ¼ cup hot water
- Ice cubes
- Blue food coloring

1 Fill the jar one-third full of hot water. Swirl it to warm the sides. Add the food coloring. Fill the upturned lid with ice.

2 Leave the ice cubes on top of the jar for a few seconds, then quickly lift the lid and squirt in some hairspray.

Escaping cloud

3 Put the lid back on. You should see a cloud start to form inside the jar. When it fills the jar completely, take off the lid and watch the cloud escape.

254 Find shapes and faces in clouds

5 MINS

Clouds constantly change shape, which is why they're wonderful to see. Lie on your back and look up at the sky. What shapes or faces can you find?

Heart in the clouds

255 Make a nature mobile

The next time you take a nature walk, bring your favorite treasures home and make them into a nature mobile. Once the mobile is complete, hang it where everyone can admire it.

What you need
- Stakes • String • Scissors
- Pebbles, cones, fossils, shells, feathers • Vines • Sticks

1 Choose two sticks or stakes of equal length. Tie them together to form an X shape. Make a hanging loop where they cross.

2 Tie objects to the stakes with string. Use single items, or tie others in chains. Arrange them so the mobile balances.

3 Form vines into loops or stars, or make pinecone animals to hang from the mobile's branches.

Pine-cone

Connected loops

Vine loop

256 Play nature tic-tac-toe

Lay out four sticks in a grid, as shown. Gather two sets of markers, such as pinecones and pebbles, find a friend, and see who is the first to get three in a row.

Take turns and try to block each other

257 Make a snail racetrack

30 MINS

Even tiny animals make choices, such as which way to turn and how fast to go. Snail racing is a fun way to see how snails move as they slide along, leaving slimy trails. Cheer them on as they cross this racetrack.

You will need
- Paint • Large piece of cardboard • Pen
- Flowerpot • Stickers
- Paintbrush
- Garden snails

1 Draw at least three different circles on the cardboard, starting with a small one in the middle—use a flowerpot or jar to trace around it.

2 Paint the circles different colors—the center is the starting point and the outermost circle is the finish line.

3 Number the stickers and put one on each snail. Put the snails in the center and watch them go! Will yours be the winner?

258 Track snails

10 MINS

Put a clay flowerpot upside down in the yard and prop up one side. The next day, take any snails out of the pot and paint a number on each one using enamel paint. Put them back in the pot. Do some return every night?

Cool, dark shelter

259 Sow seeds

Growing plants from seed is like magic—one tiny grain holds all the information inside it to create a fully grown plant. Sow seeds for your favorite plant in a recycled pot and let the magic begin!

What you need
- Seeds • Clean yogurt cups or other small containers
- Seed compost
- Trowel • Water

1 Use a pin to prick a few tiny drainage holes in the bottom of a yogurt cup. Fill the cup with seed compost.

2 Make a small hole with your finger. Insert the seed to the depth stated on the seed packet. Lightly cover with soil.

3 Gently water the seed—don't soak it too much. Keep it moist. When the seedling shows its first leaves, transplant it into a larger pot or to the garden.

> The first leaves that emerge from a seed are called cotyledons, or seed leaves. The next pair that form are the true leaves.

260 Have a sunflower-growing competition

Plant sunflower seeds in different pots. Insert stakes for support. Put height marks on each stake and see which plant grows the fastest. Challenge your friends to see who can grow the tallest plant.

Measure your flowers

261 Create a ladybug sanctuary

15 MINS

Ladybugs eat other bugs that attack plants. One ladybug may eat 5,000 aphids in its lifetime! Invite more ladybugs into your yard by building this cozy place where adult ladybugs can hibernate over winter.

1 Cut the top off the plastic bottle. Cut a piece of cardboard to roughly the same length as the bottle.

2 Roll up the cardboard as tightly as possible without crushing the ridges and put the roll inside the bottle.

3 Fill the hole in the center with twigs where the ladybugs can land. Put the bottle in a bush or other sheltered place. Slope it downward to keep out the rain.

Decoration

262 Count the spots on ladybugs

5 MINS

There are about 5,000 species of ladybug in the world. The seven-spotted ladybug is one of the most common, but some ladybugs have no spots at all. How many types live in your yard?

Red body

Black spots

263 Go pond dipping

1 HR

A pond is a whole world of life in itself, and you can discover it by going pond dipping. Just be sure to handle all the animals you find carefully, and put them back afterward.

What you need
• Dipping net
• Magnifying glass
• Pond • Shallow plastic containers

1 Once you arrive at the pond, half-fill your containers with pond water. Then you're ready to put in any finds.

2 Stand at the edge of the pond with your feet firmly balanced on the bank. Kneeling may make dipping easier.

3 Put in your net and move it in a figure-8 motion. Pull it up and turn it inside-out into a container to release your catch.

4 Take a close look at your catch with the magnifying glass. Try dipping at deeper and shallower places for different creatures.

You may be lucky and find a frog

Diving beetle

264 Tell minnows and sticklebacks apart

2 MINS

Many small fish are called minnows. You can tell a stickleback apart from them by looking for the spines that give it its name. They lie in a line along its backbone.

STICKLEBACK

Spines

Smooth back

MINNOW

265 Make a tent hideout

40 MINS

Making your own tent is fun—and if you use this design, you can take it apart and store it for use again next year. Simply assemble the two side panels and attach them. What could be easier?

What you need
- 4 x 4 ft (1.2 m) stakes
- 4 x 5 ft (1.5 m) stakes
- 4 x 6 ft (1.8 m) stakes
- Strong tape • String
- Sheet • Clothespins

Make flags for the entrance

1 Start by using two of the longest stakes to form an X for each side panel. Secure these in the middle with tape or string.

2 Put the next-longest at the top and bottom of the X. Fix these to the X stakes, then do the same for the other two sides with the two shortest stakes.

Use clothespins

3 Ask a friend to hold the sides as you fix the tops together. Make sure the entrance is wide enough! Drape a sheet over the frame and secure with clothespins.

266 Toast marshmallows

10 MINS

Toasting marshmallows on a stick is a fun thing to do if you're sitting around a campfire. Don't hold them too close—they burn quickly. Let them cool a little before eating.

267 Throw sponge bombs

10 MINS

On a hot day there's nothing better than adding water to your outdoor pursuits. Why not make these easy sponge bombs, put on your bathing suits, then see who can score the most hits?

What you need
- Large sponges in different colors
- Scissors
- Hair ties or rubber bands

1 Cut each sponge into three pieces using scissors. You need two strips from each of three sponges to make a bomb.

2 Hold your six sponge pieces in one hand. Wrap the hair tie twice around the center so that it's good and tight.

3 Pull the pieces of sponge into shape so that the colors alternate. Then soak the sponge bombs in a bucket of water and let battle commence!

It's a hit!

268 Go wave-hopping

5 MINS

The next time you're at the beach, pick a smooth, sandy spot in the shoreline and jump over the waves as they roll in. Make sure you check the depth of the water before you begin!

269 Sketch a bird

30 MINS

Drawing an animal helps you to see it in different ways. Draw a bird, for instance, and you notice things like bill shape, color, and wing stripes. If you can't get close to a real bird, you can draw one from a photograph.

What you need
- Sketch pad or drawing paper
- Pencils for drawing and coloring

1 Draw simple ovals—a large one and a smaller one—for the body and head shapes. Add some lines to represent legs, tail, and bill.

2 Look at its size: is it fat or thin? Short- or long-legged? Is the chest plain or speckled? Are the feathers long or short?

3 Study the head. Draw in the colors and patterns around the bill and eyes. Make notes of details to fill in later.

270 Draw a flight path

5 MINS

Fast wing flaps in a straight line are made by short-winged birds like ducks. Slow, steady flappers include herons, while acrobatic flight paths are made by aerial feeders like swallows.

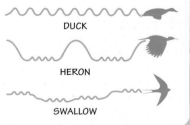

DUCK

HERON

SWALLOW

271 Make a spiderweb catcher

What you need
- 3 medium-sized straight sticks
- 1 longer, thicker stick
- String or twine

Some people are afraid of spiders, but spiders help us by eating insect pests, and they are fascinating creatures to watch, especially when spinning intricate webs. You can safely get close to one with this web catcher.

1 Make a triangle shape out of the three sticks, using the string to tie them together at the corners. Ask a friend or adult to help hold the sticks in place so that tying the string becomes easier.

Wait for a spider

2 Attach the larger stick to the triangle, tying it into place with the string. You have now created a web catcher!

Fix securely

3 In late summer or early fall, push the long stick of the catcher into the ground, near some shrubbery where you have seen spiders. Check it each morning, and you may find that one of them has spun a web inside the triangle.

272 Identify spider webs

Orb webs stretch across gaps, trapping flying insects. Radial webs have "trip-wire" strands that shake the web when touched. Large sheet webs trap crawling or flying bugs.

Orb web

Radial web

VARIOUS

Sheet web

HOUSE SPIDER

GARDEN SPIDER

273 Make a leaf collage

Collages are pictures made of different objects and materials. Colored leaves are all around in the fall. Make this leaf turkey collage, then let your imagination run wild, and create your own collage design.

1 Lay out your design first to be sure it works, then glue the first leaf onto the paper. Arrange the other leaves in a fan shape.

2 Once the fan shape—the turkey's tail—is in place, glue another leaf in the center. This will be the turkey's body.

Add eyes to finish the face

3 Use a folded leaf on top of the body for breast feathers. Glue on winged seeds for the feet and use a small seed for the bill.

274 Create land art

Designs created outdoors using natural materials are called land art. To make your own, you can use pebbles, cones, and twigs. Remember to take a photo as a record!

Land art sunburst with stick "rays"

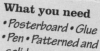

275 Make clothespin owls

Most owls don't come out until dusk, but if you have your own owls, you can enjoy them at any time of day. These little clothespin owls are easy to make and will look terrific perched around your yard.

What you need
• Posterboard • Glue
• Pen • Patterned and solid paper • Pencil
• Clothespins • Stick-on eyes • Scissors

1 Draw and cut out an owl body from posterboard. Trace the body onto the patterned paper. Cut out and glue to the body.

2 Cut out a white face and draw on two eye circles. Glue the face to the body. Stick on the eyes.

Use solid paper and add dots

3 Draw and cut out two wings and a beak from colored paper. Glue to the owl and let dry. Glue the owl to a clothespin, and perch your owl on a twig.

276 Hoot like an owl

Clasp your hands together, leaving a hollow. Put your thumbs side by side. Part your thumb knuckles, put your lips over them, and blow.

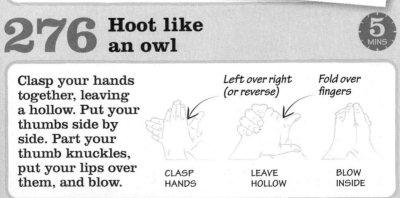

Left over right (or reverse)

Fold over fingers

CLASP HANDS

LEAVE HOLLOW

BLOW INSIDE

20 MINS

5 MINS

277 Make a sandcastle

1 HR

One of the best things about being at the beach is all the sand—it's an amazing building material. Try it out for yourself by making a sandcastle, as simple or complicated as you want. The only limit is your imagination!

What you need
- Plastic bucket and shovel
- A sandy beach
- Shells • Driftwood
- Other decorations

1 Find a good place for your castle. It should be far enough from the surf that it won't get washed away, but close enough so you can get water if you need it to wet the sand. Flatten out an area with your hands.

2 Fill a bucket with wet sand. Pack it down tightly, then turn it upside down quickly. Tap the bottom of the bucket gently and lift it off. You should have a tower.

3 Make as many towers as you like in the same way and arrange them in a castle shape. Collect shells, driftwood, even seaweed for decorations, and add a flag on top if you have one.

278 Play a game of beach volleyball

40 MINS

Divide into teams—you can have one player on each team, but two is better. If you don't have a net, draw a line in the sand. Team one serves the ball over the net. Team two has to return it within three hits.

Try to hit the ball back

279 Fill your boots with strawberries

40 MINS

You can grow scrumptious strawberries in flowerpots, but why not choose a more creative container? Recycle a pair of old rain boots into these fun planters full of delicious fruit.

What you need
- Old rain boots
- Craft knife • Gravel
- 6 strawberry plants
- Soil • Eggshells
- Petroleum jelly

1 Get an adult to cut a hole in each side of each boot. Put gravel in the bottom and fill with soil. Add a plant when you reach a hole.

2 Put a plant in the top of each boot and cover the roots with soil. Press firmly around each plant. Water both boots well.

3 Cover the top of the soil with broken eggshells and smear petroleum jelly all around the boots to keep slugs and snails away. Water your plants regularly and feed them tomato food once a week.

> Strawberries are the first fruits to ripen in early summer.

280 Harvest your crop

5 MINS

Look for berries that are fully ripe, but not beginning to rot. Pick only those that come away from their stems easily. Wash them well and enjoy!

Blackberries

281 Make a caterpillar house

Collect caterpillars in spring and summer, and watch them turn into butterflies. Remember which plants they were on—the caterpillars will eat the leaves.

1 Cut a hole in the box lid so only a rim remains. Line the box with paper towels. Spray with water. Add leaves and twigs.

2 Lift the caterpillars into the box using the paintbrush. Drape the muslin on top and put the lid on to hold it.

3 Put the box in a quiet, shady place. Change the leaves and paper every day. Make sure not to lose any caterpillars!

4 Once the caterpillars have formed pupas, don't disturb them. Soon they'll change into butterflies—at which point you should set them free.

Make sure you get the right kind of leaves

Pupa on twig

282 Hunt for insect larvae

Insects hatch from eggs into larvae before changing into their adult forms. Search for them on leaves in your yard. Ladybug larvae look armor-plated and feed on garden pests, especially aphids.

Ladybug larvae

283 Make a duck caller

Talk to the ducks at your local pond with this easy-to-make duck caller. If the sound isn't right the first time, flatten the cut end again. If using bendable straws, cut off the bendy part before making the caller.

What you need
- Drinks straw
- Scissors • Yellow, orange, and white posterboard • Glue
- Press-on eyes

1 Flatten one end of the straw by pressing on it. Cut the flat end at both sides to make a point, then press it flat again.

2 Draw and cut out a head and bill as shown. Fold back a flap at the base of the bill.

Perhaps add a feather?

Stick on the eyes

3 Glue the bill flap to the inside of the head. Insert the straw and glue the uncut end to the inside of the bill. Blow on the pointy end to go quackers!

284 Feed the ducks

Bread isn't good for ducks, but you can feed them healthy treats. Try throwing them chopped raw or cooked vegetables, thawed frozen peas, oats, birdseed, or even chopped lettuce.

285 Make a thumb-controlled watering can

15 MINS

When watering plants, a gentle stream of water is better than one big splash. This simple watering can uses your thumb to control the water flow.

What you need
- Clean plastic milk carton
- An awl or needle (ask an adult to help you)
- Bucket of water
- Waterproof decals (optional)

1 Use the awl or needle to make small holes around the bottom of the milk carton. Punch a larger hole in the center of the lid.

2 Screw the lid on tightly. Press on your waterproof decals, if using. Add as many or as few as you like.

3 Submerge the carton in water. Let it fill. Press your thumb over the hole in the top as you lift the carton. Release your thumb to water a plant.

286 Water plants

1 MIN

Aim the water at the base of the plant—some plants get diseases if their leaves become soggy. Don't oversoak plants, either. Too much water is often as harmful as too little.

Water the base

287 Search for soil insects

The soil is teeming with tiny insects, many so small you'd never notice them. With this simple funnel, though, you can discover what bugs live under your feet.

Desk lamp

What you need
- Paper towels • Wide jar • Soil
- Plastic funnel 6–7 in (15–17 cm) wide • Coarse mesh • Desk lamp

Place lamp 4 in (10 cm) above the soil

Garden soil on mesh

Insert funnel in jar

1 Dampen two sheets of paper towels, fold them, and put them in the bottom of the jar. Crumple mesh into the funnel.

2 Add garden soil and shine the lamp over it for 2 hours.

3 The heat from the light will cause bugs in the soil to move through the mesh into the jar. See how many you've collected, then let them go.

288 Distract an ant

Find an ant trail in your yard. Put a sugar cube to one side of the trail. See how long it takes the ants to find the sugar. Try this with different groups of ants. Which finds the bait the fastest?

White sugar

Brown sugar

Ants follow scent

289 Grow a sack of potatoes

You can use containers of all kind—even bags—as planters. Add soil and you can even harvest potatoes. You need "chitted" seed potatoes, which means that the eyes have started producing shoots.

What you need
- Seed potatoes
- Trash-can liner with drainage holes in a burlap sack • Trowel
- Potting compost

Chitted eyes

Egg carton

1 Fill the liner one-quarter full with compost. Roll down the bags to soil level. Add three potatoes, eyes-up. Cover thinly with compost and water.

2 Water whenever the soil looks dry. As they grow, cover the shoots with compost once a month for three months.

3 Unroll the bags as the level rises. After about 90 days, split the side of the bag open and harvest your delicious potatoes.

290 Potato printing

Cut a potato in half. Draw a shape on it with a marker. Ask an adult to cut away the flesh with a knife, so the shape is raised. Pour paint onto a plate, press the shape in it, then stamp it onto paper.

Printed stamp

Raised star shape

291 Create sunflower people

Fill your yard with sunflower people and bring a smile to your borders. Turn paint cans into bodies and pick out a face when the seed heads form for some fantastic and friendly plants.

What you need
- Old paint cans with holes in the bottom • Paint • Soil
- Markers or pens • Gravel
- Plastic bags with holes in the bottom • Sunflower seeds

Remove seeds to make a face

1 Draw or paint "bodies" on the cans. When dry, line cans with a bag. Add a layer of gravel, then fill with soil. Plant a seed ½ in (1 cm) deep in each. Water well.

2 Put a plastic bag over each can, but remove the bags when leaves appear. When flowers form, remove all flowers except the top one.

Body

292 Harvest sunflower seeds

Wait until the petals start to drop and the seeds start to loosen. Cut off the flower heads and rub the seeds with your hand. Dry them before storing.

Dried petals

Ripe seeds

293 Make corn-husk paper

Don't throw away your corn husks—use them instead to make paper that is just like the papyrus used by the ancient Egyptians. Ask an adult to help!

What you need
- Corn husks • Washing soda
- Large stainless-steel pot
- Flour-and-water paste • Old dish towel • Rubber gloves
- Paper towels, newspapers

1 Fill a pan with water, and stir in 1 tbsp washing soda per quart (liter) of water. Add the husks and simmer for 30 minutes.

2 Wear rubber gloves. Rinse the husks in cold water. Lay them flat, and let drain on paper towels. Pat them as dry as possible.

3 Put some husks ridge-side down, overlapping the edges. Brush with flour paste, then put more husks on top, ridge-side up, at right angles to the first.

4 Lay an old dish towel on top, add newspaper, and weigh everything down with a heavy object until dry. Paint the paper and use it to decorate a notebook.

294 Grow corn

10 MINS

Fill a container with potting soil. Sow dried corn kernels ½ in (1.5 cm) deep. Water regularly and leave to sprout for 7–21 days.

Corn leaves

EAR

295 Catch some tadpoles

Tadpoles are the first life stage of frogs and toads. The most common are frog tadpoles, hatched from eggs (spawn) laid in spring. Look for them in nearby ponds or ditches.

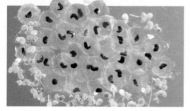

1 When they are laid, the eggs are surrounded by a cloudy jelly. Frogs lay eggs in clumps, and toads lay eggs in strings.

2 Put some pond water in the jar and container. Look for tadpoles among the water weeds.

Spot the tadpole!

3 Put the net in the water under the tadpoles and swiftly lift it up. Quickly put them in the jar, then into the container.

296 How old is your tadpole?

5 MINS

Tadpoles become frogs or toads in 16 weeks. After six weeks, tiny back legs appear. By nine weeks, the arms bud and the tadpole looks more like a frog. The tail shrinks to a stump by 12 weeks.

Long back legs

Still has tail

TEN-WEEK-OLD TADPOLE

297 Create a tornado in a glass

Tornadoes form when hot and cold air masses collide and start to rotate, creating a funnel-shaped cloud that causes enormous damage when it hits the ground. Make your own tornado with this easy experiment.

Add glitter to simulate debris

What you need
- Tall drinking glass • Water
- 2 tsp vinegar • Glitter
- 2 tsp dishwashing liquid
- 2 drops blue food coloring

1 Fill a glass three-quarters full with water.

2 Add the vinegar, soap, and food coloring.

3 Swirl or stir the mixture in a circular motion. Watch the tornado appear. Add some glitter to simulate debris and see how that affects the tornado.

Blue tornado

Clear water

End of funnel

298 Make an ocean in a bottle

Fill a clean plastic bottle half-full with water. Add blue or green food coloring and shake well. Then add a little vegetable oil. Screw the cap on tightly. Rock the bottle back and forth and watch the ocean waves roll.

299 Weave a plant-pot teepee

20 MINS

Decorate a plant pot with a teepee and you'll add color to the yard that everyone can enjoy. Use colored string, thin floral wire, raffia, or a combination—just make sure whatever you choose is waterproof.

1 Push the three bamboo stakes into a large pot so that they form a tripod shape. Tie them together at the top with twine or wire.

2 Attach a long piece of string or wire to the top of the teepee and weave it in and out of the stakes until you reach the base. Either tie it off to a stake or wrap it around the top of the pot to add even more color.

Put some flowering plants around the base

3 Repeat with as many different-colored strands as you like. When you're happy with your design, plant flowers or climbing vines around the base for added decoration.

300 Divining for water

10 MINS

Divining is an ancient way of finding water. Loosely hold a forked stick parallel to the ground. Concentrate on water. If the end suddenly points down, you've found it!

Focus your thoughts on water

301 Make a sundial

1 DAY

The Sun brings life to planet Earth, keeping us warm and helping plants grow. Make this simple sundial, however, and you can also use the Sun to tell the time—no batteries or watches required!

What you need
- Flowerpot • Glue
- Red, orange, and yellow posterboard
- Long dowel rod
- Modeling clay • Scissors

1 Draw a Sun with rays on yellow posterboard. Cut it out. Glue a circle of posterboard to the back for support.

2 Cut out red and orange rays and glue them between the yellow rays so that the colors alternate—red, yellow, orange.

3 Cut a hole in the center. Push the dowel through it, then through the flowerpot's hole. Fix it to the pot with clay.

4 Put the sundial in the sun. At noon, position the dial so that the shadow falls across one ray. Mark this as 12 o'clock. Mark every hour until sunset, then repeat at dawn to mark all the morning daylight hours.

Rod should be at least 8 in (20 cm) above the pot

Line of shadow tells the time

Alternate colors of rays

302 Cook with the Sun

15 MINS

Fry an egg with sunshine. The temperature needs to be at least 95°F (35°C) for it to cook. Heat a frying pan on a hot sidewalk, then break an egg into it. Watch and wait!

The egg will cook if hot enough

303 Plant some daffodil bulbs

15 MINS

Flowers like tulips, daffodils, and crocuses grow from bulbs. Plant a dwarf species like these daffodils in late December, and in just eight weeks you'll have a pot full of blooms to give as a gift.

What you need
- 5 in (12 cm) plant pot
- Narcissus Tête-à-Tête (mini-daffodil) bulbs
- Gravel • Trowel
- Compost • Water

1 Cover the bottom of the pot with gravel. This will allow water to drain away slowly.

Lush green leaves

Flowers give off fragrant scent

2 Half-fill the pot with the potting compost. Lay a few bulbs on the soil. Cover them with compost and water gently.

3 Put the pot in a dark place for six weeks. Remember to water it from time to time. When shoots appear, move the pot into the light.

304 Watch a carnivorous plant

30 MINS

Carnivorous plants like the Venus flytrap feed on insects. If you see one, look for the tiny hairs inside its leaves. If a bug touches one, the leaves will snap shut and slowly digest the unlucky victim.

Damselfly

Stiff fringes prevent bug from escaping

305 Spot constellations in the night sky

30 MINS

In ancient times, people grouped stars into constellations to help find their way at night. Many were named after legendary figures and animals. Find a star map, wait for a clear night, and see how many you can find.

What you need
- Clear, starry night
- Star map or atlas
- Binoculars or a small telescope (optional)

Betelgeuse
ORION

1 Orion the Hunter is easy to spot in both hemispheres because it's one of the largest figures in the sky. Look for three bluish stars in a diagonal line that form his "belt," then look up from those to the bright red star, Betelgeuse, that marks his shoulder.

2 Leo the Lion is another easy one to find. The stars that make up its head and chest form a sickle shape, like a reversed question mark. You can often spot planets here, too.

3 Use your star map to help you locate other constellations, such as the Big and Little Dippers (or Bears) and Cassiopeia.

LEO

306 Find Venus

3 MINS

Look west, just after sunset, and you'll see a very bright, white-looking "star" in the sky. This is actually the planet Venus. It's so bright you can sometimes see it in the daytime.

Venus rising

307 Plant a window box

20 MINS

Even if you don't have any outside space, you can plant a window box garden. Choose plants that flower at different times of year, and you'll always have something pretty to look at. The bees will thank you, too!

What you need
• Window box with drainage holes, plus tray • Gravel • Trowel • Compost • Flowering plants • Watering can

1 Put the box on its tray in your chosen position. Put a thin layer of gravel in the bottom. Add compost. Take the plants out of the pots.

2 Put in your plants, adding in soil to their surface level. Fill in any spaces with more compost. Water them well.

Daisies

Pansies

Busy lizzies

308 Make a mini nature reserve

20 MINS

Plant a window box with bee-friendly plants such as lavender, or rosemary and ivy, where insects can shelter. Add a dish of water so tiny creatures can drink or bathe in it.

Add a dish of water

309 Make a foil riverbed

What you need
- Aluminum foil
- Garden hose
- Items that float

You can make your very own "river" in your backyard. All you need is a long length of aluminum foil and some water. Float bottle caps or containers, or make your own nutshell boats (see below) to race.

Have a race with some walnut-shell boats

1 Unroll 16 ft (5 m) of aluminum foil. Lay it out flat in the yard or patio (ask permission first)—wherever you want your river to flow. Smooth out any bumps underneath. Point the end toward a flower bed or vegetable garden so that the water isn't wasted while you play.

2 Carefully fold the sides up to make walls about 2 in (5 cm) high. These will form your riverbanks.

3 Put a garden hose at the top and turn it on just at a trickle. Wait for the water to flow. See how many different things you can float down it.

310 Make walnut-shell boats

Put a tiny ball of clay in the bottom of walnut-shell halves. Carefully push a toothpick through a leaf or piece of paper to make a sail. Push the toothpick into the clay to serve as a mast.

Paper sails

311 Make a pirate ship

40 MINS

Build a pirate ship from a foil food container and construction paper. Once it's assembled, you can paint it any color you like. Make sure to add sails. Don't forget the skull and crossbones!

What you need
- Clean foil container
- Craft sticks • Scissors
- Paper • Egg carton
- Paint • Cork • String
- Wrapping paper • Glue

1 Push the front of the foil container into a point to make the hull. Cut construction paper to size for the decking.

2 Make cuts around the deck so you can fold it in to fit the hull. Glue it in place.

3 Use the egg carton lid for the bridge. Make two masts from craft sticks and glue to the boat. Cut out a wheel and glue it onto a cork to form the base.

Add sails and rigging

Fix wheel to cork with tack

312 Make a pirate flag

1 HR

Cut out a rectangle of black fabric. Cut a skull and crossbones from white felt and glue it on. Draw eyes, a nose, and a mouth in black marker. Glue the flag to a small stake.

Flag glued on

Small stake

313 Make a fake fossil

40 MINS

Real fossils can take millions of years to form, but you can make a real-looking "fossil" in one day with this project. Use a shell, a handprint, a toy, or an actual fossil.

What you need
• Modeling clay • Water • Petroleum jelly • Posterboard strip • Item to fossilize • Plaster of Paris • Small plastic container • Yellow or red food coloring

1 Shape modeling clay into a thick, flat disk. Rub petroleum jelly on top. Press your object into the clay, then take it out.

2 Push the posterboard strip into the modeling clay around the mold. Mix the plaster and color it with a few drops of food coloring.

A real ammonite was used here

3 Let the plaster thicken, then pour it into the mold. Let it set for a day. Carefully remove your "fossil." Use it as a paperweight.

314 Look for shaped stones

10 MINS

The next time you're at a pebbly beach, search for shaped stones. Heart shapes are fairly easy to find, but look carefully enough and you may find other familiar shapes.

STONE HEARTS

315 Grow beans in a glass

10 MINS

Roots go down and shoots go up and you don't usually get to watch them do it. Plant beans in a glass, though, and you can see how plants grow. It's a fast, fun way to get your bean plants going.

What you need
- 2 glasses or glass jars • Paper towels
- Bean seeds • Water

First leaves

Bean falls away

1 Put some bean seeds in a glass, fill it with water, and let the beans soak overnight.

2 Fill another glass with damp paper towels. Put the soaked beans midway down the side of the glass.

3 After 2–3 days, the beans should sprout, or "germinate." Remember to keep the paper moist.

Roots take in water

316 Plant a bulb in water

5 MINS

Fill a hyacinth vase with water to below the base of the bulb. Put the bulb on top. Place it in a dark place for 8 weeks. Keep refilling the water. When the bulb shoots, bring it into the light.

Shoots grow upward

Bulb shouldn't touch water

317 Calculate a tree's height

Have you ever wondered how tall a nearby tree is? Grab a friend and a stick and find out. If your measuring tape is too short, measure in stages and add everything up for the total height.

1 Face the tree. Hold the stick straight out in front of you. Move closer or farther away until the stick top is level with the top of the tree and the trunk-base lines up where you're holding the stick.

2 Get your friend to stand by the tree, facing you, so that his or her feet are level with the base of your stick. Turn the stick through a 90 degree angle to your right. The stick base should still be lined up with the tree base.

3 Have your friend walk away from the trunk toward the left. Stop him when he reaches the end of the stick. Measuring that distance will give you the tree's height.

Hold the stick as level as possible

318 Make a tire swing

Ask an adult to help you. Find an old tire and tie a length of strong rope securely around it. Tie the other end to a sturdy branch. Be sure you can reach the swing easily from the ground.

You can sit inside or on top

319 Grow a bug-eating bottle garden

20 MINS

Make an alien mini-world—the plant in the jar is an insect-eating sundew. Put it on a sunny windowsill and watch how any bug that touches its dewy "hairs" gets stuck fast.

What you need
• Aquarium gravel
• Plastic jar • Glitter
• Carnivorous plant compost • Sundew
• Modeling clay

Modeling clay alien

1 Put a layer of colored gravel in the jar. Add a layer of compost and press it down gently.

2 Plant the sundew in the compost and firm it in. Scatter gravel on top. Add a modeling-clay alien. Look out, bugs!

320 Discover a lost world

20 MINS

Fill a tray with a thin layer of gravel, add a thick layer of compost, and plant small ferns and palms. Water them, then add some toys and dinosaurs.

Paradise palm

Dinosaur model

321 Make a pooter

Handling insects can be tricky; some can bite, pinch, or sting. A good way to collect them is to use an insect "pooter." It works by suction, which you provide. But don't worry—you won't swallow any bugs!

What you need
- Glass jar • Plastic tubing • Muslin or gauze • Rubber band • Cardboard • Pencil • Tape • Modeling clay

1 Cut two plastic tubes: one 20 in (50 cm) long; one half that. Fix muslin over one end of the shorter tube with the rubber band.

2 Trace around the jar lid on cardboard; cut out. Make two holes. Tape the cardboard to the jar. Push the tubes into the holes and attach with clay.

3 Put the end of the long tube over a bug and suck sharply on the short tube. This will pull the bug into the jar. Study your insect—then release it.

322 Shake a tree to find bugs

3 MINS

Line a baking sheet with white paper. Place the baking sheet under a shrub or tree branch, then shake the branch and see what insects tumble out.

Stick for shaking

Bugs fall out

323 Put together a naturalist's kit

30 MINS

A naturalist is someone who not only looks carefully at the natural world, but also records those observations and learns from them. You can put together a kit and make your own discoveries!

What you need
- Backpack • Notebook
- Pencils • Insect net
- Magnifying glass
- Binoculars • Tape measure • Penknife

1 Use a light backpack for essentials. Find one with outside pockets so you can carry things like water bottles (for you) and collecting bags (for your specimens).

2 Binoculars will help you see far-away creatures such as birds or squirrels, while a magnifying glass takes you into the tiny world of insects.

3 Pack a notebook and pen to write down or draw your observations. A small ruler or tape measure is handy, too, as is a small insect net. Don't forget to use your own senses— they're the most important tools of all.

NOTEBOOKS

NET

MAGNIFYING GLASS

PENKNIFE

TAPE MEASURE

BINOCULARS

324 Follow a snail trail

5 MINS

It's easy to find a snail— just look for a silvery, shiny trail of slime on the surface of a leaf, the sidewalk, or a plant pot. See if you can trace it to the snail itself.

Slimy snail trail

325 Make a windmill flower

20 MINS

Find out which way the wind blows with this bright windmill flower. Add posterboard leaves to its stem and plant it in a flowerpot.

Windmill "petal"

What you need
- Squares of colored posterboard
- Scissors • Double-sided tape
- Tape • Thumbtacks • Stick

Put tape in the center

1 Make four diagonal cuts almost to the center. Fold in each corner and stick to the tape.

2 Cut a flower-shaped center and push a tack through both it and the center into the stick.

3 Make some leaves and tape them to the stem. Loosen the tack if the windmill doesn't turn.

Green posterboard leaves

326 Use CDs to scare crows

15 MINS

To keep birds from eating your plants, punch holes in plastic bottle caps. String them up on stakes next to some old CDs and hang them in the garden.

Stake supports

Bottle tops and CDs

327 Build a bivouac

A bivouac is a shelter or hide made from whatever is available—sticks or branches, with ferns or straw to provide cover or help you hide away. Here's an easy way to make your own bivouac.

What you need
- 1 long and several shorter branches or sticks • String, twine, or vines
- Ferns or straw

1 Find a stick that's at least as long as you are tall. Tie two shorter sticks together, as shown, to support the long stick.

2 Lean other sticks all along the long stick on alternating sides to make a tentlike shape.

3 Cover the bivouac with long grasses, ferns, bracken—anything you can find that will camouflage you and provide shelter. Then try it out for size!

Straw and grass

328 Roll down a hill

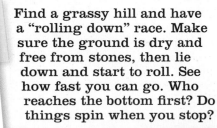

Find a grassy hill and have a "rolling down" race. Make sure the ground is dry and free from stones, then lie down and start to roll. See how fast you can go. Who reaches the bottom first? Do things spin when you stop?

329 Force buds to open

When trees start to show buds after a long winter, you know that spring is finally on its way. Encourage buds to break into leaf a bit sooner by bringing some twigs indoors. Try forsythia, horse chestnut, willow, or birch twigs.

What you need
- Twigs • Jar
- Water • Pruning shears

Buds begin to break out

1 Ask an adult to help you cut a twig with some pruning shears. Always ask permission first and don't take too much.

3 Keep the jar in a sunny spot and wait for the buds to open. This could take a few weeks.

2 Make sure the bottoms of the twigs are cut at a slant and place them in a jar of water.

Slanted cuts help stems take up water

New leaves

330 Look for catkins

Many spring-flowering trees produce their flowers in the form of catkins, which appear before the leaves. Take a walk to look for catkins on hazel, birch, willow, or alder trees.

Alder catkins

331 Investigate a fallen log

Nothing is wasted in nature. Look closely at a fallen log, and you'll see that it is home to hundreds of tiny creatures—and other plants and fungi. Observe this essential habitat, but do your best not to disturb it.

What you need
- Sketchbook
- Pen or pencil
- Digital camera
- Magnifying glass

1 Look at the outside of the log. Does it seem like it has been here long or is it newly fallen? Is the bark whole or crumbly?

2 Look closer at the log's surface. Do you see holes or spider webs? Lift a piece of bark—are there patterns in the wood?

Has an animal made holes in the log?

3 See if there are any signs of animal activity or tracks around the log. Note down any plants or animals you find, or take photos to identify later.

> Fallen logs are often known as "nurse logs" because they provide a sheltered spot for other seedlings to grow. The rotting material also adds nutrients to the soil.

332 Log your log

20 MINS

Make a log or journal of all the living things you find on or near a fallen log. Revisit your log from time to time to see whether anything has changed. Is something new living there?

CENTIPEDE

FERN

FUNGI

LARVAE

333 Make a nature ice bowl

Ice keeps drinks cool, but did you know you can also make things out of ice? With a few kitchen items and some flowers, you can create a stunning ice bowl. Serve dessert in it—or just enjoy it while it lasts!

What you need
• 2 freezer-proof bowls, one smaller than the other
• Flowers and leaves
• Tape • Fork • Water

Use a jar to hold down the inner bowl

2 Fill the space between the bowls with water. Add flowers and leaves, spacing them out with a fork. Freeze for 10 hours.

Make this bowl with berries and fruit slices and use it to hold lemonade!

1 Fill the large bowl with 1 in (2.5 cm) of water and put it in the freezer until hard. Place the smaller bowl on top. Tape it in place.

Leaves and flowers

3 Remove the tape and turn the bowls upside down. The ice bowl should slide out, ready to use. It will last for several hours.

Ice

334 Create an ice lantern

You can make a lantern in the same way using half a plastic bottle as the base and a plastic cup to hollow out the middle. Add leaves, twigs, or ivy, and freeze solid. Turn out the lantern, add a tealight, and enjoy the glow.

Red berries

Fir twigs

335 Keep a Moon diary

As the Moon circles the Earth, it seems to change shape as it moves in and out of the Earth's shadow—from a full circle to a thin crescent. Watch the Moon every night for a month, and you can chart all of its phases.

What you need
- Pen • White and black paper • Scissors
- Compasses • Glue
- Aluminum foil
- Binoculars

1 Draw a chart with 29 squares on a large piece of white paper. Cut out 29 black paper circles and glue one in each square.

2 Look at the Moon on a clear night. Cut out the Moon's shape in foil and glue it to the first black circle on your chart.

3 Repeat this process every night for one month. Use binoculars if you like, but they aren't essential. If it's cloudy, simply leave that circle blank.

336 Go night walking

1 HR

Moonlit wood
Flashlight

Take a flashlight and an adult on a night walk and see what animals you can find. You might see bats or owls, or hear crickets calling or foxes barking.

337 Make a home for a frog or toad

Toads and frogs like a cool, damp, shallow burrow to hide away in during the day and to hibernate in over winter. You can make them welcome in your yard by building them a special home.

What you need
- Trowel • Clay pot
- Damp leaves
- Watering can
- Collected rainwater

1 Find a cool, moist place in the shade. Dig a hole with a trowel, making the hole a bit longer than the clay pot.

2 Place the pot on its side in the hole. Bury about half of it by filling the inside with moist soil.

A cozy bed

3 Use damp leaves to make a nice bed for the frog or toad inside the pot, and water the area to keep the pot in place.

338 Find a frog— or is it a toad?

1 HR

Toads have dry, warty skin and are usually brown or beige. Frogs have smooth, damp skin that can vary in color, and they often have a pale or white neck area.

Smooth skin

Warty skin

FROG

TOAD

339 Build a bee hotel

Some bees find holes in trees or walls to use as nests. The hollow stems of the bamboo in this bee hotel will give them somewhere for their young to grow.

What you need
- 20 pieces of bamboo stake—½ in (1 cm) in diameter, 6 in (15 cm) long
- Scissors and strong tape
- Modeling clay • Clay pot

1 Stand the pieces of stake (or hollow plant stems) on end to make a bundle. Use the tape to bind them together.

2 Press the stakes firmly into a lump of modeling clay to seal one end.

Leave in a sunny, dry spot

3 Put the stakes into the pot with the open ends facing outward. Use more modeling clay to wedge the bundle tightly inside the pot.

340 Count different types of bee

15 MINS

There are about 20,000 different bee species in the world. Most are solitary types that live alone and don't make honey. Social bees live in colonies. How many species can you spot?

Solitary bee

Social bee

MASON BEE

BUMBLEBEE

341 Make a stepping-stone path

Make your own stone path by molding concrete into nature-shaped "stones." Find some really big leaves (rhubarb or sunflowers are good), but ask permission first. ⚠

What you need
- Disposable gloves
- Plant leaves • Cement mix
- Putty knife • Sand • Trowel
- Apron • Large plastic tub
- Big pieces of cardboard

1 Wearing gloves and an apron, mix the cement in the tub. Lay a leaf face-down on the cardboard. Cover with 1½ in (4 cm) cement. Smooth it over.

2 After two hours, turn the stone over and peel off the leaf. Let dry for two days. Arrange the stones into a path.

3 Outline each stone with a trowel, lift, and dig out the soil beneath. Add a thin layer of sand and put the stone on top.

342 Plant a herb path

Liven up a walkway by planting herbs in gaps between the stones. Choose plants like chamomile for a fragrant path, or colorful herbs for a rainbow effect.

Stone slab

Low-growing herb

343 Test a bird's brain

How smart are birds? Test them with this simple puzzle. Offer tasty treats in two pots—one closed, one open—and find out whether the birds in your yard are smart enough to figure out how to open a lid.

What you need
- 2 identical plastic pots • Cardboard or stiff paper • Pencil
- Scissors • Tape
- Pebbles • Birdseed

1 Half-fill one pot with pebbles to weigh it down, then top it off with birdseed. You'll do the same with the second pot later.

2 Trace around the second pot onto the cardboard. Cut out the shape, leaving a tab.

Birds eat from open pot first

3 Fill the second pot like the first. Tape the lid on one side. Put both pots close together. When the open pot is empty, which birds lift the lid to get the seed?

344 Identify birdsong

Birdsong tells you which birds are nearby. When you spot a bird singing, make a note of the sounds you hear, and you'll soon learn which birds makes which songs.

Chshree-ip
Schrree-eew
Shrr-ooo

Use lines to note whether the songs go up or down

345 Make a scarecrow garden buddy

1 HR

This weird, wonderful figure will keep birds away from your plants. Use cans to make his arms and legs, and a plastic bottle for his body. Add a scary face to really put the birds off!

What you need
- Cans, plastic pots, caps • Garden wire
- Coathanger
- Glue • Scissors
- An adult to help!

1 Join two cans by threading wire through a hole made in the bottom. Cross the wires. Twist into loops to join. Make four sets.

2 Use a plastic bottle for the body. Push two pieces of a coathanger through it. Loop the ends and hang a limb off each.

3 Use a plastic pot for the head and glue on bottle caps and foil to make a scary face. Wire it to the body, and hang up your buddy.

Add hands and feet

346 Make a traditional scarecrow

45 MINS

Stuff old clothes full of straw for the limbs and body and tie off the arm and leg ends with string. Stuff a pillowcase for the head. Mount on a wooden pole frame and add a hat!

Glue on a face

347 Make a wind chime

40 MINS

A garden isn't just about plants—it should appeal to all your senses, including hearing. This easy wind chime will make a gentle, soothing "tink tink" whenever the wind blows. You probably already have all you need to create it.

What you need
- Terra-cotta pot with drainage hole
- String • Plastic container lid
- Beads, small pebbles, or shells

Shorter strings should hang at pot level

Central string

1 Tie a long piece of string to a branch. Cut a large hole in the center of the container lid, and eight holes around the edge. Tie a shorter string to each hole.

2 Thread the long string through the lid and the pot. Attach a bead big enough to block the hole in the pot.

3 Knot four lid strings to the central string to hang the lid above the pot. Tie a pebble, bead, or shell to the ends of the other four lid strings.

348 Paint a pebble paperweight

30 MINS

Choose a smooth pebble the size you want your paperweight to be. Paint it all over in a background color. After it has dried, mark out your design with a pencil or chalk, then fill in the colors.

Dotted design

349 Make a bird-feeder box

30 MINS

Birds are some of the easiest wild creatures to attract to your yard, and watching them is lots of fun. Make this simple milk-carton box feeder, fill it with seed, and watch the birds flock to it.

What you need
- Clean milk carton
- Brown, green, and yellow plastic bags
- Scissors, glue, stapler
- Wire • Twigs • Birdseed

1 Cut a hole in the side of the carton about 2 in (5 cm) from the bottom. This will form the feeder's entrance hole.

2 Cut leaf shapes from plastic bags and glue them to the carton. Make tiny drainage holes in the bottom of the feeder.

3 Staple the top closed. Thread wire through a hole at the top. Poke a twig just below the door to make a perch. Fill the feeder with seed and hang it.

350 Monitor your bird feeder

5 MINS

It's amazing how many birds visit a feeder when wild food is scarce. See how many birds of different species you can count on your feeder. Note down the figures, and see how they change at different times, and from one day to the next.

Raw nuts

Food level

Coal tit

Blue tit

351 Grow salad on your wall

25 MINS

Even if you only have a patio, you can still grow good things to eat. Just attach some empty plastic bottles to a sunny wall to make this summer salad garden.

What you need
- Clean plastic milk bottles • Craft knife
- Seed compost • Trowel • Lettuce seeds • Nails or hooks • Hammer

1 Ask an adult to help with the first two steps. Cut the bottoms off the bottles. Then put a few drainage holes in the caps, and screw them back on.

2 Use a hammer and nails to attach the containers to a sunny wall. Position them so you can reach to water them easily.

3 Fill the containers with seed compost. Sow your seeds. Choose cut-and-come-again lettuce or arugula. Water well. In dry weather, water daily.

352 Make cress eggheads

20 MINS

Carefully wash out some boiled-egg shells and let dry. Draw faces on the shells and put them into egg cups. Fill with compost, add cress seeds, and watch the green "hair" grow!

Cress "hair"

353 Go beachcombing

1 HR

You never know what you'll find on a beach. One day it could be a whole scallop shell, another day you could find fossils. Go on a beach walk and see what the tide has brought in for you.

What you need
- Sunglasses
- Beach footwear
- Beach bucket or a bag to hold your finds

1 Get started early—the best finds go to the first people on the beach.

2 Look along the tide line, but also check farther back. Sometimes the wind blows perfect shells away from the surf.

3 Get your feet wet. You can find great shells in the surf. Also try hunting after a storm when the tide is out.

4 Take only what you really want and can easily carry. Don't disturb any live creatures, and take all litter home.

SEA SNAIL

SCALLOP

SPONGE

SEAWEED

SEA URCHIN

DRIFTWOOD

354 Make a sand face

10 MINS

Use the beach as your artist's palette and make a face out of sand, shells, pebbles, driftwood, or anything else you can find. Or simply draw one in the sand with a stick. Make it as big as you like—the tide will wash it away.

Pebbles make a great nose

355 Make a compost heap

40 MINS

Left to itself, nature is a top recycler, but if you want to give nature a hand, build a compost heap. You'll not only reduce the amount of garbage going into landfills, but your garden will also get some great free compost, too!

What you need
• An old wooden crate
• Brown-layer items—twigs, paper, dry stems, hair
• Green-layer items—grass clippings, fruit and vegetable peels

1 Choose a site for your compost container. The best is on bare soil in a sunny place. Ask an adult to help you build a simple box out of scrap wood if you don't already have a box or crate that's large enough.

2 Start your heap by adding dry "brown" layers—shredded newspapers and dry straw are ideal. Add a layer of "green" items on top. Alternate the layers so you have half green and half brown.

3 Don't add cooked food, fish, dairy, or meat products—they will attract mice. Turn your heap with pitchfork every few weeks. After a year, your compost should be ready to use.

Keep a 50/50 mix of "green" to "brown" items

356 How hot is your heap?

20 MINS

You can check that your compost heap is working by taking its temperature. Insert a long thermometer into the center of the heap. If it reads 104–122°F (40–50°C), then your heap is breaking down at the correct rate.

Check the temperature

357 Make a twig vase

30 MINS

Transform a plastic cup and some sticks into this artistic vase. Add colorful twine and an evergreen sprig, then fill it with flowers for a woodland gift.

What you need
- Plastic yogurt cup
- Dark paper • Pruning schears
- Double-sided tape • Twine
- Twigs • Glue • Scissors
- Rubber band

Plastic cup

1 Cut a piece of paper long and wide enough to wrap around the cup, covering it nearly to the top. Fix it in place with the tape.

2 Ask an adult to help you cut the twigs slightly taller than the cup. Glue them around the sides. Use a rubber band to hold them in place.

3 Once the glue dries, tie some raffia or colored twine around your vase and secure it with a bow. Add a sprig of evergreen for decoration.

358 Make a shell plant pot

15 MINS

Put a plant, still in its own container, inside a larger clear plastic plant pot. Fill between the two pots with seashells so that the inner pot can't be seen.

Shells hide inner pot

359 Make a leaf-stencil bag

45 MINS

The natural world contains many beautiful designs. Why not stencil one of them onto a cloth bag? Leaves work particularly well for this project, and you can use more than one shape, if you like.

1 Trace around your chosen leaf on a piece of stencil paper. Ask an adult to help you cut out the shape with the knife.

2 Cut sponges into 2–3 pieces. Put fabric paint on the plate. Dip a sponge piece into the paint and stencil it on paper to practice.

3 When you're ready, slip a piece of wax paper inside the bag to stop the paint from bleeding through, then sponge your stencils onto the bag.

360 Make leaf prints

20 MINS

Use leaves as stamps to make cards, book covers, or wrapping paper. Brush a layer of paint over a leaf surface, press it down on paper, and smooth with your hand before lifting it off.

Sycamore

Oak

361 See sunspots

20 MINS

To us, the Sun looks like a large, yellow disk in the sky. Occasionally, dark sunspots appear on its face. You should never look at the Sun directly, so try this safe way to view them.

What you need
- Two large pieces of heavy cardboard
- Binoculars • Paper
- Tape • Pencil
- Scissors

1 Cut two holes near the top of one piece of cardboard to hold the eyepieces of the binoculars. Prop the cardboard up on a chair. Insert the binoculars and cover one lens.

2 Position a chair facing the Sun. Place the other piece of cardboard about 3 ft (1 m) in the shade behind it. Focus the binoculars to get a sharp image.

3 Put the paper on the screen and draw around the Sun. Mark any dark sunspots you see.

362 View an eclipse

15 MINS

You can use the same sunspot technique to view an eclipse, which happens when the Moon passes in front of the Sun. Eclipses are rare, but they are always a popular news item, so look out for one near you.

Moon passing across the Sun

363 Watch a newt grow

If you're lucky enough to have a nearby pond and spot a tadpole with a "frill" behind its head, it's a recently hatched newt. Why not monitor the pond and watch one of these fascinating amphibians grow up?

What you need
- Access to a pond that contains newts

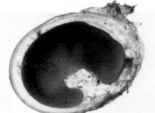

1 Unlike frogspawn, newt eggs are laid individually. Look for a single egg wrapped in a submerged leaf.

2 A newly hatched newt eats its yolk sac, then feeds on tiny plankton. The feathery bits on either side of its head are gills.

3 After a few weeks, the minnowlike newtlet grows legs and begins to look like its parents. It can leave the water about 10 weeks after hatching.

364 Listen to frogs

If you're outdoors in spring or summer and there's water close by, listen to see if you can hear frogs calling. Some make a deep, throaty croak, while others, such as tree frogs, sound almost like crickets.

Expanded vocal sac makes sounds louder

365 Play bird bingo

The next time you have friends over, why not challenge them to a game of bird bingo? Set up the playing cards in advance, then go outside, watch for birds, and see who's the first to make a complete line.

What you need
• Paper • Ruler
• Scissors • Glue
• Pen or pencil
• Pictures of bird behavior

First full line wins!

DRINKING PREENING PERCHING

FLYING PECKING BATHING

LANDING SWIMMING SINGING

Write in each behavior

1 Make playing cards with nine squares on each card. Go online to find images of birds doing different things.

2 Print the pictures, cut them out, and glue one in each square. Use a different order for each card.

3 Write in each behavior below its matching picture, to make sure everyone knows what to look for.

4 Give each player a card and a pencil. Go outside and watch bird behavior. The winner is the first to cross off a line— or to check off the whole card.

Is it a leap year?

A year with 366 days in it is called a leap year. We need to add an extra day every four years to keep the calendar in check with the time it takes Earth to circle around the Sun. Leap years are associated with frogs so why not try one of the froggy activities in this book to mark the 366th day of the year, or have a game of leapfrog!

Index

Acknowledgments

Dorling Kindersley would like to thank the following for their assistance in producing this book: Alison Gardner for props; Anna Hall, Charlie Noon, Anna Reinbold, Ina Stradins, Duncan Turner, and Francis Wong for design assistance; Karen Shooter and Jemima Dunne for assistance with photoshoots; Claire Bowers, Claire Cordier, Laura Evans, Lee Thompson, Romaine Werblow, and Rob Nunn for archive and picture research; Adam Stoneham for preproduction assistance; Vanessa Davies, Ria Osborne, and Howard Shooter for photography; Julie Dent for shoot location; and Izzie and Polly Alexander, Oliver Ansell, Olivia Banks, Ben and William Bristow, Alfie Chan, Kit Davies, Jesse and Alex Dent, Finlay Horastead, Isabella Linnane, Anjana Nair, Christine Ni, Erin and Samuel Regan, Kaiya Shang, Chloe, Oliver, and Luke Shooter, Henry and Oliver Tompsett, Ruby Vincent, Jorja and Mia Walsh for modeling. Also, from the Delhi office, Nand Kishore Acharya for DTP assistance, and Sumedha Chopra for compiling picture credits. The publisher would like to thank Claire Thomas at the RSPB for reviewing all the pages.

The publisher would like to thank the following for their kind permission to reproduce their photographs:

(Key: a-above; b-below/bottom; c-center; f-far; l-left; r-right; t-top)

123RF.com: Marilyn Barbone 82cr, Chris Brignell 82cl, 82br, Sergey Galushko 23br, paulrommer 175bc, Darya Petrenko 101bl, Yann Poirier 82tl; **Alamy Images:** Juniors Bildarchiv / F314 197crb, Stephen Chung 156br, Simon Colmer 187cl, Paul Gapper 125b, Hemis 113br, Phototake Inc. 77bl, Photoshot 197clb (Soldier beetle), 197cb, Antje Schulte—Spiders and Co. 69br, Tony Watson 66bl; **Corbis:** Marilyn Angel Wynn / Nativestock Pictures 110br, Daniel Attia 144bl, Ed Darack / Science Faction 158br, Warren Faidley 65br, Ingolf Hatz 82tr, Radius Images 158cl, Morgan Petroski / Albuquerque Journal 186br, Visuals Unlimited 111br; **Dorling Kindersley:** Batsford Garden Centre and Arboretum 12-13 (Background also for 20-21, 28-29, 36-37, 44-45, 52-53, 60-61, 68-69, 76-77, 84-85, 92-93, 100-101, 108-109, 116-117, 124-125, 132-133, 140-141, 148-149, 156-157, 164-165, 172-173, 180-181), Lucy Claxton 7br, Jerry Young / Jerry Young 197clb, Thomas Marent / Thomas Marent 25cl, Natural History Museum, London 17cb, 32crb, 32bc, 109br, 197tl, 197tl (Red Admiral), RHS Hampton Court Flower Show 2012 20tr, Rough Guides 17br, 120b, 128bl, 177 (Grass background for steps 1,2,3), Jerry Young 136br; **Dreamstime.com:** Ajafoto 52bl, Patrick Allen 131bl, Angelamaria 129b, Deosum 99br, Dule964 6-7 (Background also for 14-15, 22-23, 30-31, 38-39, 46-47, 54-55, 62-63, 70-71, 78-79, 86-87, 94-95, 102-103, 110-111, 118-119, 126-127, 134-135, 142-143, 150-151, 158-159, 166-167, 174-175, 182-183), Sonya Etchison 147bl, Eric Isselee 199c, Isselee 197bc, Kai Koehler 139bl, Robyn Mackenzie 6 (Paper on all spreads), Mikelane45 51br, Juriah Mosin 123br, Nomadimages 63cl, Mohamed Osama 25, Prentiss40 51tl, Rachwal 188cl, Sergei Razvodovskij 6-7 (Background also on 10-11, 14-15, 18-19, 22-23, 26-27, 30-31, 34-35, 38-39, 42-43, 46-47, 50-51, 54-55, 58-59, 62-63, 66-67, 70-71, 74-75, 78-79, 82-83, 86-87, 90-91, 94-95, 98-99, 102-103, 106-107, 110-111, 114-115, 118-119, 122-123, 126-127, 130-131, 134-135, 138-139, 142-143, 146-147, 150-151, 154-155, 158-159, 162-163, 166-167, 170-171, 174-175, 178-179, 182-183, 186-187), Alfio Scisetti 83br, Srekap 127bl, Val Thoermer 173bl, Topaz777 132bl, Witr 187cra; **FLPA:** Robert Canis 32cb, Steve Young 140cla; **Fotolia:** Jacek Chabraszewski 28bl, Thomas Dobner / Dual Aspect 180br, Maksym Dykha 97br, Eric Isselée 197clb (backswimmers); **Galaxy Picture Library:** Robin Scagel 158cla; **Getty Images:** Glowimages 87c, Kick Images / iStock Exclusive 63 (wood), 74cla, 74cra, 82tl (wood background), 94cla, 94cra, 94cl, JGI / Jamie Grill / Blend Images 164br, Charles Krebs / The Image Bank 197cl, Digital Vision / Ricky John Molloy 153cra, 153cl; **Nature Picture Library:** Adrian Davies 32br (Wild cat droppings); **naturepl.com:** Adrian Davies 32br, Alex Hyde 197tc, Rolf Nussbaumer 197c; **Pearson Asset Library:** Studio 8 135cla, 135cra, 135cl, Gareth Boden 87cr, MindStudio. 87cl, Tudor Photography 87cb, 181br, Coleman Yuen 63crb, 188c; **rspb-images.com:** Chris Gomersall 88br; **Science Photo Library:** Luke Dodd 76cla, European Southern Observatory 173cb, Thomas Heaton 94br, John Sanford 76cra, 76cl, 76cr, Barbara Strnadova 38br, 197cra

All other images © Dorling Kindersley

For further information see: **www.dkimages.com**